Soups & Stews

One-Dish Meals

Kay Shaw Nelson

HENRY REGNERY COMPANY · CHICAGO

Library of Congress Cataloging in Publication Data

Nelson, Kay Shaw.
  Soups & Stews.

  1. Soups.   2. Stews.   I. Title.
TX757.N44   641.8'13   74-6900
ISBN 0-8092-8392-1

Copyright © 1974 by Kay Shaw Nelson. All rights reserved
Published by Henry Regnery Company, 114 West Illinois Street
Chicago, Illinois 60610
Library of Congress Catalog Card Number: 74-6900
International Standard Book Number: 0-8092-8392-1
Manufactured in the United States of America

Contents

To my daughter,
Rae Katherine Nelson,
a convivial dining companion

INTRODUCTION

One snowy winter evening, while browsing through some books, I came across a marvelous salutation: "For soups and stews and choice ragouts Nell Cook was famous still."

Taken from the Ingoldsby Legends, a series of tales told by a parson under an assumed name and later discovered in the family chest, this tribute to Nell intrigued me. For even in 1842 when the Reverend Richard Barham had penned those lines, there must have been a proper appreciation for these delectable dishes.

Not knowing Nell's repertoire of recipes that had so impressed the parson, I set out to compile my own cosmopolitan collection of them. In particular I relished those one-pot or one-meal nourishing dishes of which even the plainest can be a creative combination, pleasing to both the eye and the palate. From my wanderings in various parts of the world I had not only acquired a great fondness for and appreciation of these dishes, but also a formidable number of recipes.

Of infinite variety and flavor, soups and stews have no geographical boundaries. Each of the world's cuisines has some choice offerings. Many are robust and hearty familiar creations while others are refined unknown dishes with foreign names. On the other hand, we think of ragouts as belonging to the French, and like much of their cookery, consider them a little more special than other stews. They are perfect for special-occasion meals.

While soups, stews and ragouts are age-old favorites they have particular appeal for the contemporary cook. Utensils, for example, are simple. All you need is a pot or kettle, some spoons and knives, and depending on how intricate the preparation, perhaps a few helpful gadgets. Most kitchens have all the necessary equipment.

Shopping for the ingredients poses no great problem as most items are readily available at the nearby supermarket. And in times when all of us are concerned about food prices, these one-dish meals can well be considered as boons to the budget. No worthy dish can be put together for a few cents, but in comparison to other choices, these selections can be prepared without investing considerable sums. Most of the fare is good and honest and is improved by seasoning and slow cooking. Even the more expensive ones will "go further" because of the type of cookery they are.

Preparation time can vary from several minutes to an hour or more, depending on the recipe. But, with few exceptions, all of the work, including the cooking, can be done ahead and the dish either kept in the refrigerator or frozen. Soups and stews reheat beautifully. For some there are "last minute" additions such as vegetables and egg yolks or other thickeners. Even so, these are no great effort.

Soups, stews and ragouts will appeal to carefree cooks who want to welcome and mingle with guests, if entertaining, or have time with the family before the meal. None of the dishes suffers terribly if left on the stove a few minutes longer than planned.

With dishes like these you do not need much else on the menu. Some type of bread is usually a good accompaniment, along with a salad or vegetable. Appetizers or first courses are optional; desserts can be purchased or easily made. To aid in meal planning a menu suggestion is given with each recipe. Generally, this type of fare generates an air of conviviality and the meal is thus relaxed and pleasurable.

There is no magic or mystique about cooking soups, stews and ragouts. All that you need is some time and effort for which you will be well rewarded. To assist in the preparation and cooking of these dishes, some helpful hints are offered in forthcoming pages. A glossary appears at the back of the book.

Throughout the book the recipes have been planned to provide fare that is not only appealing, but which is an interesting variation on the usual culinary repertoire. Some dishes are familiar; others are not. In serving them the cook may not acquire the fame of Nell Cook, but she will receive the warm appreciation of those who are bound to enjoy soups, stews and ritzy ragouts.

SOME HELPFUL HINTS

Although it is sometimes difficult to make distinctions between soups, stews and ragouts, there are some basic differences in these substantial dishes.

Generally speaking, a hearty soup is made by cooking meat, poultry, seafood and/or vegetables in a seasoned liquid. The ratio of liquid to solids is customarily more than in a stew or ragout. Also the liquid is generally thinner, similar to a broth. A thickening agent, however, is sometimes used after cooking. Soups are almost always cooked on the top of the stove and do not necessarily simmer for a long period of time.

Stews are made by covering the food with liquid and cooking in a tightly covered heavy pot or casserole at a low temperature, either in the oven or over direct heat. The cooking is generally lengthy as the purpose is to tenderize the foods and to make them more palatable by retaining the juices. Meat stews are either brown or white. For the former the meat is browned before cooking in liquid, while for the latter it is not. Stews are generally quite thick, containing rich sauces derived from the slow cooking or from the addition of thickening agents.

1

Ragouts are more complicated and fancier variations of stews, and are usually of French origin. Generally they are highly seasoned and often include wine.

Raw Materials

Necessary ingredients for soups, stews and ragouts will, of course, vary according to the recipe. One general rule applies to the selection of all of them. The finer the quality of foods and liquids, the better the dish. This does not necessarily mean the most expensive choices, but it is advisable to take time to select fresh food that is in prime condition. There are substitutes available for broths, stocks and bouillons, but those made from scratch will add much more flavor to the dish. If wine is used, it too should be of good quality.

The cuts of meat used for these dishes are often less tender and less expensive, such as beef shank, neck, shin, brisket, short ribs, flank and chuck; veal breast, shoulder, and shank; pork loin and shoulder; and lamb breast, neck, shoulder and riblets. These cuts will require longer cooking than poultry, seafood and vegetables.

Most of the essential ingredients can be easily found in supermarkets and neighborhood groceries, but for some recipes it may be necessary to obtain items at specialty food stores.

Cooking Equipment

Soups, stews and ragouts can be made in a variety of pots, kettles, baking dishes or casseroles. The size will vary according to the recipe. Generally the cooking utensil should be heavy and large, with a tight-fitting cover. It should be determined whether the dish can be used for cooking over direct heat (or on top of the stove) as well as in the oven. Some utensils are suitable for both types of cookery; others are not.

A large kettle or French *marmite* can be used for making broths and stocks. Soups can be cooked in a large saucepan, kettle or Dutch oven, with a cover, and with a capacity of 6 or more quarts.

For stews and ragouts it is desirable to have a flame-proof, heavy-bottomed pan, kettle or casserole. Pans made of heavy copper or enamelled cast iron are best as they retain the heat during long, slow cooking and the food will not burn. Other good ones are made of stainless steel with a base of some metal such as copper. There are also utensils of earthenware, pottery, Pyrex, and other heat-proof materials that are oval, round or rectangular. Some of these, however, cannot withstand direct heat. Special dishes that can be purchased in some department stores or gourmet shops include the French enamelled cast iron *cocottes* and earthenware or metal *daubières*.

Other necessary equipment includes knives and wooden boards for chopping, can or jar openers, measuring cups and spoons, a beater or whisk, a sieve or strainer, mixing bowls, skillets, one or more large cooking spoons, a slotted spoon or skimmer, a long-handled fork, a garlic press, a food mill and a larding needle.

Preparation and Cooking

For the best results, great care should be accorded the preparation and cooking of each dish. Some will take longer than others, but most of the work can be done beforehand. It is up to the cook whether she wishes to make her own stock or broth and cut up the meat. These preparations involve time and effort, but many persons prefer to do them. While it is not difficult to cup up most meats, cleaning and cutting fish and poultry is a little more messy and complicated. Thus, this can be done by the butcher or fish dealer. The preparation of vegetables and other ingredients does not generally present any great problems.

Some recipes call for marinating the meat in a seasoned liquid to tenderize it. Others suggest larding lean cuts by inserting strips of fat into the flesh with a larding needle. The latter will increase the juiciness of the meat. If the meat is to be browned, it should be wiped dry or it will steam instead. Add only a few pieces at a time and keep the pieces separate while browning. Do not pierce the meat with a fork while it is cooking or desirable juices will escape. After a preliminary browning, some stews are deglazed by flaming alcohol, such as brandy, before the addition of the liquid and other ingredients.

The most important step in stewing meat or other foods is to dissolve the food juices into the heated liquid in which they are cooked. Thus the first step in the cooking of a stew is very important. The liquid should be slowly brought to a simmer, just so that it bubbles occasionally, and then left to cook as slowly as possible. This is important because if the liquid boils the meat will become tough and not taste properly. All meat shrinks while cooking, but lower temperatures reduce the loss. The length of the cooking time will vary for the type and cut of meat, but the best way to be sure that it is properly done is to test it. It is not possible to give precise cooking times. Those in the recipes are to be used as guide lines.

Vegetables and other ingredients are added to soups and stews at various intervals during the cooking. Generally they require less time than meats and should not be overdone as they will lose their shape and color. To improve the flavor of some stews, vegetables or other seasonings are first sautéed in fat.

Once a stew has cooked, it is necessary to remove any fat that has collected on the surface. This may be done with a slotted spoon, skimmer or pieces of paper toweling while the liquid is still hot, or the dish may be cooled and refrigerated and the solidified fat lifted off.

For some stews it may be necessary to correct the final sauce by thinning it with more stock, wine or other liquid. It can be thickened by boiling down or adding *beurre manié* (tiny balls of flour and butter), cornstarch, arrowroot, or egg yolks and cream. If a stew is refrigerated or frozen, it is advisable to adjust the sauce after it has been reheated. These dishes are not difficult to reheat, but should be checked so that none of the ingredients becomes overdone and lose its proper form and color.

Flavorings

Most of the dishes in this international collection are flavorful well seasoned creations that are designed to conform as closely as possible to the taste prevalent in their place of origin. Thus garlic and onions are liberally added to dishes from Mediterranean locales and sour cream and dill are featured in those of Eastern Europe. Ginger and soy sauce appear often in many of the Oriental recipes. The cook may wish, however, to alter some of these flavorings by using lesser amounts, such as one instead of two cloves of garlic or a smaller quantity of chili powder. This is her option. It is also helpful to know that various brands of some flavorings will vary in strength. This is especially true for curry powders and soy sauces. It is preferable to taste each dish to determine the desired flavor.

A wide variety of herbs and spices is used in soups, stews and ragouts. These should be added with caution as a small amount may go a long way. If it is necessary to substitute dried herbs for fresh ones, remember that the latter are less pungent. As a guideline, use 1/2 teaspoon of a dried herb to replace each tablespoon of a fresh one.

Freezing

Many of the dishes in this collection can be satisfactorily frozen. In fact, in some cases the cook may wish to double or triple the ingredients so that what is not needed immediately can be put in the freezer.

If dishes are to be frozen, be careful not to overcook them as each will undergo additional cooking when reheated. It may be advisable to shorten the specified time by five or ten minutes.

In order to save space, stocks and broths can be boiled down to concentrates. Using the concentrate for flavoring, additional liquid can be added later. Cooked foods and liquids to be frozen should be cooled quickly and thoroughly and then put into appropriate containers, leaving an inch at the top to allow for expansion. Some baking dishes can be used for freezing and then transferred directly to the stove for re-heating. Soups may be stored for about six months and stews from two to four months, depending on the ingredients.

It is advisable to add some foods to these dishes after they have been defrosted and reheated. Among them are potatoes, dumplings, pasta and vegetables such as green peppers, green peas, lima beans and corn. Try to season a particular fare lightly so the seasonings can be checked and corrected after reheating. If a liquid is to be thickened with *beurre manié*, add this also after the dish is reheated and just before serving.

Frozen dishes may be thawed at room temperature or by placing the containers under running hot water. Reheat over low heat in a covered dish on the top of the stove or in a moderate (325°F.) oven. Frozen food can be slowly reheated without thawing but, of course, this takes longer.

Bouillons, Broths and Stocks

Many recipes for soups and stews call for the use of bouil-lons, broths or stocks. These terms are often used inter-changeably, since all three are produced by the same basic cooking process, boiling solid foods in seasoned liquids. The primary distinction is that bouillons and stocks are richer and more concentrated, the solid ingredients having been cooked to the point of discard, whereas broths are cooked for a shorter period and the solid foods are still usable.

In making stocks and bouillons, meat, poultry, fish or vegetables are slowly simmered in seasoned liquids. Bones are generally included in most of them as they provide neces-sary strength and gelatin. During the very slow cooking process all the nutrients and flavors are extracted from the solid foods. The selection of the ingredients, therefore, is very important and should include those which contain the necessary elements. The flesh of older animals contains more flavor than that of younger ones. Red meats yield more taste than white. Seasoning, particularly with salt, must be done carefully or the end product will acquire an undesirable flavor. After cooking, the remnants of the solid ingredients are discarded, and the remaining liquid must be properly degreased and, in some cases, clarified.

Broths are also acquired by simmering foods in seasoned liquids, but the process is not as lengthy nor is the aim to extract all the goodness from the ingredients, which are sometimes served in the broth.

Today it is not absolutely necessary to go through the time and effort of making one's own bouillon, stock or broth. Supermarkets carry ample supplies of beef bouillon and chicken broth, in either canned, powdered or tablet form, and canned or bottled clam juice is a good substitute for fish broth. These can easily be kept on hand. Concentrated bouillon liquid and cubes, however, are not recommended for long, slow cooking as they make the dish too salty. The homemade products are always superior in flavor and body, however, and can be made in large quantity and stored in the refrigerator or freezer to be used as needed.

Recipes for several of the basic liquids follow.

Brown Stock (or Bouillon)

2 pounds marrow bones, cracked
4 pounds shin or neck of beef, cut in small pieces
12 cups cold water
1/2 cup chopped celery
1/2 cup diced carrots
1/2 cup chopped onion
1 medium bay leaf
3 parsley sprigs
1/4 teaspoon dried thyme
1/4 teaspoon dried marjoram
6 whole cloves
8 peppercorns, bruised
1 tablespoon salt

Brown stock will have a richer color if the bones and/or meat are browned first. There are two methods of doing this. One is to put the cracked bones in a preheated hot oven (450°F.) for about 25 minutes, turning once or twice, or until well browned. They are then put in a large kettle with the other ingredients. The other is to scrape the marrow from the bones and put it in a large kettle. Then the marrow is heated and half of the pieces of meat browned in it. Add the bones, remaining meat and water. Put over moderate heat and bring slowly to a simmer. With a spoon or skimmer, take off all the foaming scum that has risen to the top. Add the remaining ingredients and bring very slowly to a simmer. Leave over very low heat, partially covered, for about 3 hours, or until all the possible goodness has been extracted from the ingredients. Stir occasionally while simmering. When the cooking is finished, strain the liquid and degrease it. This may be done by letting the stock settle for about 5 minutes and then removing the fat with a spoon, skimmer or paper towel. Or the stock can be cooled and put in the refrigerator until the fat hardens. Then it may be lifted or scraped off the top. The stock can be kept in the refrigerator or put in containers and frozen or may be frozen in freezer trays to produce cubes. If kept in the refrigerator for several days, it should be brought to a boil every day or so. Makes a little over 8 cups.

White Stock

Substitute cracked veal bones and veal knuckle or shank meat for the marrow bones and beef in the Brown Stock recipe.

Chicken Stock (or Bouillon or Broth)

1 stewing chicken, 4 to 5 pounds, cut up
12 cups cold water
1/3 cup each of diced carrots, celery and onions
1 leek, white part only, cleaned and sliced (optional)
2 sprigs parsley
1 small bay leaf
1/2 teaspoon dried thyme
2 teaspoons salt
6 whole peppercorns, bruised

Wash and wipe dry the chicken and put in a large kettle. Add the water and slowly bring to a simmer. With a spoon or skimmer remove any scum. Add the vegetables and seasonings and simmer very gently, covered, about 2½ hours. While simmering occasionally remove any scum. Strain. Remove the fat on the surface with a spoon or skimmer. Cool and put in the refrigerator until the fat hardens on the surface. Remove the fat and strain again. Store in the refrigerator up to 5 days or pour into containers and freeze. Makes a little over 8 cups.

Note: The chicken can be discarded or used for hash or other dishes.

Fish Stock

2 pounds white-fleshed fish with bones and trimmings
8 cups cold water
1 medium-sized onion, peeled and sliced thinly
1 medium-sized carrot, scraped and sliced thinly
2 whole cloves
1 bay leaf
1/2 teaspoon dried thyme
4 parsley sprigs
1 teaspoon salt
10 white or black peppercorns, bruised
1/2 lemon, sliced

Put all the ingredients in a kettle. Bring slowly to a simmer and skim. Cook very slowly, uncovered, for 1 hour. Strain and cool. Refrigerate or pour into containers to freeze. Makes about 6 cups. (1/2 or 1 cup of dry white wine and/or 1/3 cup of chopped mushroom stems can be added to the ingredients, if desired.)

SOUPS

In the realm of hearty and nourishing soups, there is a galaxy of tempting creations from which to choose for everyday and company meals. Whether termed a bisque, *sopa*, chowder, *corba*, potage, *zuppa* or plain pot, each is fun to prepare and delightful to savor.

Soup is superb for every occasion. "Soup meals" are fun at brunches and luncheons. They are great suppers or informal dinners and easily can star at late evening parties. A bowl of soup is good served out-of-doors, on the porch, in the kitchen or at the dining room table. Both children and adults relish the pleasure of partaking of the savory contents of a pot of homemade soup.

Perhaps the greatest compliment that can be paid to soup is its long-lasting appeal, for the saga of soup dates back to the beginning of cookery when ancient man discovered the idea of filling an empty animal-skin bag with meat, bones and liquid, along with hot stones to cook the mixture. With the invention of clay containers the ingredients became more varied and were simmered over direct heat. Thus was created the first *pot au feu*, or pot on the fire.

10

An early literary reference to soup is found in the Bible. In Genesis one can read that Esau sold his birthright to his brother Jacob for "a pottage of lentils." Over the centuries cooks have utilized the available bounty of land and sea to create a lengthy repertoire of national favorites, each prepared and flavored according to local taste.

We are indebted to soups not only for the establishment of the first restaurant but for the word itself. In 1765 an enterprising Parisian soup vendor, one Boulanger, began advertising his menu items as "magical" *restaurants* (restoratives or pick-me-ups). Not only was his business successful but his soups became the rage of Paris.

Soups have long been reliable friends, the mainstay at many tables through good and bad times. Settlers in the New World would have been lost without them. On their historic voyage the Pilgrims subsisted primarily on soups prepared in large pots suspended from overhead beams of the Mayflower. In the kitchens of the early colonists the predominant cooking utensils were kettles, filled most often with nourishing soups to sustain the families.

When more lavish fare became available and lengthy meals of many courses were stylish, robust soups were relegated to the unworthy status of common fare. But, thankfully, fashions in gastronomy change, and now, marvelous pots of soup, the old favorites of our forefathers and from around the world, once again hold places of honor on our tables.

In planning soup menus remember that the suggested portion in a recipe is a highly negotiable subject, for the amount will vary according to what else is served and the appetite of the diner. Therefore the number of servings is offered merely as a guideline. The suggestions, however, are on the generous side. It is better to have too much soup than too little. And it can always be reheated and enjoyed another time. With each recipe is a suggested menu that includes a soup as a main dish, one or more accompaniments and dessert. A first course or side dishes can easily be added, if desired.

Soup should be served as attractively as possible. Sometimes it can be offered from the pot in which it was cooked. But it is particularly delightful when ladled from a colorful tureen, as Alice discovered in Wonderland:

"Beautiful soup, so rich and green
Waiting in a hot tureen!
Who for such dainties would not stoop?
Soup of the evening, beautiful soup."

Gulyás Soup

The national stew of Hungary, *gulyás*, which means herdsman's pot, is a paprika-flavored dish of many variations. A thinner version is *gulyás leves*, goulash soup, and should be made with deep orange-red Hungarian paprika, the finest kind. This is a good dish for a winter luncheon or supper.

4 medium-sized onions, peeled and chopped
2-3 garlic cloves, crushed
6 tablespoons lard or bacon drippings
3-4 tablespoons paprika, preferably Hungarian
3 pounds beef chuck or round, cut into 1-inch cubes
2 large carrots, scraped and diced
2 large tomatoes, peeled and chopped
8 cups water
salt, pepper to taste
4 medium-sized potatoes, peeled and cut into small cubes

Sauté the onions and garlic in the lard in a kettle over low heat until tender. Stir in the paprika and cook for 1 minute. Add the beef cubes, several at a time, and brown on all sides. Add the carrots, tomatoes, water, salt and pepper. Bring to a boil. Lower the heat and simmer, covered, for 1 hour. Add the potatoes and continue to cook for about 30 minutes longer, or until tender. Serves 8 to 10.

MENU

Gulyás Soup
Pumpernickel
Warm Apple Strudel

Spanish Quarter-of-an-Hour Soup

This is a delectable seafood soup that appears frequently on Spanish restaurant menus. Supposedly it can be made in a quarter of an hour but the name is misleading. Even though it takes somewhat longer, the result is well worth the effort. It is a good luncheon dish.

1/3 cup diced ham or bacon
1-2 tablespoons olive oil
1 medium-sized onion, peeled and chopped
1-2 garlic cloves, crushed
1 large tomato, peeled and chopped
1 teaspoon paprika
6 cups chicken broth or bouillon
2 cans (8 ounces each) minced clams, undrained
1/2 cup uncooked rice
salt, pepper to taste
1 cup fresh or frozen green peas
1 cup cleaned small or medium canned shrimp
2 hard-cooked eggs, shelled and chopped
strips of canned pimiento

Combine the bacon or ham, oil (use 1 tablespoon if bacon is used and 2 tablespoons for ham), onions and garlic in a large kettle. Sauté them over low heat for 5 minutes. Add the tomatoes and paprika and sauté about 3 minutes longer. Pour in the broth and clams, with their liquid, and bring to a boil. Stir in the rice. Season with salt and pepper. Lower the heat and cook over medium heat, uncovered, for 15 minutes. Add the peas and shrimp and cook 10 minutes longer if the peas are fresh, 5 if frozen. Serve garnished with the eggs and pimiento. Serves 8.

Note: Cleaned fresh shrimp may be used. Sauté them with the onions until pink and then spoon out and set aside. Return to the soup 5 minutes before removing from the heat.

MENU

Spanish Quarter-of-an-Hour Soup
Sliced Orange and Onion Salad
Crisp Crackers
Chocolate Soufflé

Mediterranean Lamb-Lentil Pot

Since ancient times dried lentils have been staple fare in most of the Mediterranean countries. They are highly prized for their nutritional value and are used interestingly in soups, each well seasoned to local preference. This one includes other favorite local foods—lamb, garlic, onions and tomatoes. It is a good supper dish.

4 lamb shanks, about 3½ pounds total
salt, pepper to taste
2 tablespoons (approximately) butter or margarine
1 large onion, peeled and chopped
1 garlic clove, crushed
1 can (1 pound, 12 ounces) tomatoes, undrained
1/2 teaspoon dried thyme
1 medium-sized bay leaf
3 parsley sprigs
1 cup dried lentils, washed and drained
8 cups water
2 tablespoons fresh lemon juice
1/3 cup chopped fresh parsley

Trim the shanks of any excess fat. Discard the fat. Rub the shanks with salt and pepper. Heat the butter in a large kettle. Add the shanks and brown on all sides. Remove to a plate. Add the onion and garlic to the drippings, adding more butter if needed, and sauté over low heat until tender. Add the tomatoes, thyme, bay leaf, parsley sprigs, and season with salt and pepper. Cook 1 minute, breaking the tomatoes with a spoon while cooking. Return the shanks to the kettle.

Cook slowly, covered, for 1 hour. Add the lentils and water and continue to cook slowly, covered, about 30 minutes longer, or until the ingredients are tender. Add the lemon juice and chopped parsley and remove from the heat. Take out the shanks and cut all the lamb from them. Return the lamb to the soup. Remove and discard the bay leaf and parsley sprigs. Reheat if necessary. Serves 6 to 8.

Note: This soup is even better if cooked beforehand and reheated.

MENU

Mediterranean Lamb-Lentil Pot
Hot Garlic Bread
Fresh Fruit Compote

Swiss Onion-Cheese Soup

This is an easy-to-prepare soup made with two favorite Swiss foods, onions and cheese. An excellent dish for a week-end luncheon.

6 medium-sized onions, peeled and sliced
6 tablespoons butter or margarine
8 cups beef bouillon
2 cups grated Emmentaler, Gruyère or Swiss cheese
freshly grated nutmeg, salt, pepper to taste
6 slices toasted French bread

Separate the onion slices and sauté them lightly in the butter in a large saucepan or kettle. Add the bouillon and bring to a boil. Lower the heat and stir in 1½ cups of the cheese, the nutmeg, salt and pepper. Cook over very low heat, covered, about 15 minutes, until the cheese melts. To serve, place a slice of the toasted bread in each of six soup plates. Ladle the soup over it. Sprinkle with the remaining cheese. Serves 6.

MENU

Swiss Onion-Cheese Soup
Herbed Tomato Salad
Bread Sticks
Warm Apple Tarts

Potée Lorraine

In France there are a number of thick and substantial soups that are called *potées*, generally meaning that they are cooked in an earthenware pot. Especially good is this regional soup of Lorraine featuring pork, beans and cabbage.

2 cups dried kidney beans, washed and drained
1 large onion, peeled and chopped
4 medium-sized carrots, scraped and chopped
3 medium-sized leeks, white parts only, cleaned and sliced
2 tablespoons lard or bacon drippings
1 smoked boneless pork butt, about 2 pounds
bouquet garni
(3 parsley sprigs, 1 bay leaf, 1/4 teaspoon dried thyme,
wrapped in cheesecloth)
1 garlic clove
3 whole cloves
salt, pepper to taste
4 sweet potatoes, pared and cut into medium-sized cubes
4 medium-sized turnips,
pared and cut into medium-sized cubes
3 cups shredded green cabbage
12 cups water

Put the beans and 6 cups of water in a large saucepan and bring to a boil. Boil for 2 minutes. Remove from the stove and let stand for 1 hour. Sauté the onion, carrots and leeks in the lard in a large kettle over low heat until tender. Put the pork butt in the center of them. Add 6 cups of water, the *bouquet garni*, garlic clove, whole cloves, salt and pepper. Bring to a boil. Lower the heat and cook slowly, covered, for 30 minutes. Add the beans and liquid in which they soaked and continue to cook slowly for 1 hour. Add the sweet potatoes, turnips and cabbage and continue to cook slowly for 1 hour, perhaps less, until the ingredients are tender. Remove and discard the *bouquet garni*, garlic clove and whole cloves. Take out the pork and slice as thickly as desired. Serve separately or return to the soup. Serves 10.

MENU

Potée Lorraine
French Bread
Peach Ice Cream on Wine-Soaked Peaches

Jamaican Pepper Pot

A classic dish of the West Indies is a highly seasoned stew called a pepper pot. In Jamaica, however, a pepper pot is a thick soup featuring a number of native vegetables, pork and beef, and seasonings varying from mild to spicy. This recipe is an adaptation.

2-3 ounces salt pork, diced
1½ pounds short ribs of beef, cut into 3-inch pieces
1½ pounds stew beef, cut into 2-inch cubes
12 cups water
1/2 teaspoon dried thyme
salt, pepper to taste
1 large onion, peeled and finely chopped
1-2 garlic cloves, crushed
2 green onions, with tops, cleaned and sliced
2 tablespoons vegetable oil
1 large green pepper, cleaned and chopped
1 package (10 ounces) fresh spinach, washed and trimmed
1 package (10 ounces) fresh kale, washed and trimmed
1 can (15½ ounces) okra, drained

**4 medium-sized (about 1½ pounds) sweet potatoes,
peeled and cut into chunks
1 medium-sized potato, peeled and cut into
medium-sized cubes**

Put the salt pork and short ribs in a large kettle and brown the ribs on all sides. Add the stew beef and brown on all sides. Pour in the water and slowly bring just to a boil. Remove any scum. Add the thyme, salt and pepper and lower the heat. Simmer, covered, for 1 hour, occasionally removing any scum that rises to the top. While the meat is simmering sauté the onion, garlic and green onions in the oil in a skillet until tender. Add the green pepper and sauté for 1 minute. Remove from the heat and set aside. After the meat has cooked for 1 hour, add the sautéed vegetables and the other remaining ingredients to the kettle. Continue to cook slowly, covered, for about 30 minutes, or until the vegetables and meat are cooked. Remove from the heat and cool slightly. Take out the short ribs and cut off and discard any fat. Cut up the meat into bite-sized cubes and return to the kettle. Reheat, if necessary. Serves 8.

MENU

Jamaican Pepper Pot
Warm Banana Bread
Mixed Chopped Fresh Fruit
Macaroons

Near Eastern Yogurt-Meatball Soup

In the Near East many of the most inviting dishes are flavored with yogurt, a staple food. This dish illustrates what an appealing flavor yogurt can impart to two other regional favorites, meatballs and rice.

**1 pound ground beef
1/2 pound ground lamb**

1 medium-sized onion, peeled and minced
3 eggs
2 garlic cloves, crushed
2 tablespoons chopped fresh dill or parsley
salt, pepper to taste
12 cups beef bouillon
2/3 cup uncooked rice
2 cups plain yogurt
juice of 1 large lemon
1/4 cup chopped fresh parsley

Combine the ground beef and lamb, onion, 1 egg, garlic, dill, salt and pepper in a large bowl. With a spoon or the hands, work to thoroughly combine the ingredients. Shape into small balls about 1 inch in diameter. Set aside. Heat the beef bouillon in a large kettle until it boils. Drop in the meat-balls and add the rice. Stir well and lower the heat. Cook slowly, covered, until the meatballs and rice are tender, about 30 minutes. Stir in the yogurt. Mix together the remaining 2 eggs and lemon juice in a small bowl and stir in 1 cup of the hot broth. Mix well and stir into the soup, beating constantly while adding. Leave over low heat, stirring, until thickened. Stir in the parsley. Serves 8.

Note: If the soup is prepared beforehand, do not add the yogurt, the mixture of eggs and lemon juice and parsley until just before serving.

MENU

Near Eastern Yogurt-Meatball Soup
Sesame Seed Bread
Baklava or Fresh Fruit

Sopa Mallorquinas

This inviting vegetable soup is from the lovely island of Majorca, the largest of the Balearic Isles in the western Mediterranean. The cuisine, akin to that of Spain's Catalan province, is highly seasoned and rich.

**1 cauliflower, about 1½ pounds
1 large Bermuda onion, peeled and sliced thinly
3 medium-sized leeks, white parts only,
cleaned and sliced thinly
2 medium-sized garlic cloves, crushed
3 tablespoons olive or vegetable oil
4 large tomatoes, peeled and chopped
6 cups water
1 medium-sized bay leaf
1/2 teaspoon dried thyme
salt, pepper to taste
2 medium-sized raw potatoes,
pared and cut into small cubes
slices of crusty white bread**

Cut the stem and tough outer leaves from the cauliflower. Wash in cold running water and drain. Set aside. Sauté the onion, leeks and garlic in the oil in a large kettle over low heat until tender. Add the tomatoes and sauté 2 minutes. Place the whole cauliflower over the sautéed vegetables, and add the remaining ingredients, except the potatoes and bread. Bring to a boil. Lower the heat and cook slowly, covered, for 20 minutes. Add the potatoes and cook about 20 minutes longer, or until the cauliflower is tender. Break into flowerets before serving. Ladle over slices of bread in wide soup bowls. Serves 6.

MENU

*Sopa Mallorquinas
Chocolate Ice Cream and Almond Slivers*

Cajun Shrimp Bisque

The French-speaking descendants of the outcast Nova Scotians, who made their way to the bayou country of Louisiana some 200 years ago, are called Cajuns. Their cookery is fascinating and includes several well seasoned seafood dishes, particularly those made with crayfish and shrimp. This is a good luncheon soup.

8 cups water
1 medium-sized lemon, sliced
bouquet garni (1 bay leaf, 3 sprigs parsley,
1/4 teaspoon dried thyme)
salt, pepper to taste
2 pounds raw unshelled shrimp
1 cup finely chopped onion
1 garlic clove, crushed
9 tablespoons butter or margarine
1 can (14½ ounces) whole tomatoes, undrained
and chopped
1 can (10½ ounces) tomato purée
1/2 teaspoon dried oregano
5 tablespoons all-purpose flour
1 cup light cream or milk
few drops Tabasco sauce

Put the water, lemon slices, *bouquet garni*, salt and pepper in a large kettle and bring to a boil. Add the shrimp and cook over moderate heat, covered, about 5 minutes, if shrimp are not frozen, and 8 to 10 minutes if frozen. Do not overcook. Remove from the stove. Strain and reserve the liquid. Let the shrimp cool until they can be handled. Peel and remove the veins; set aside. Sauté the onion and garlic in 4 tablespoons of butter over moderate heat until tender. Add the tomatoes and tomato purée, and continue to cook 5 minutes longer. Pour in the strained broth and add the oregano. Cook slowly, covered, for 15 minutes. While cooking, combine the remaining 5 tablespoons of butter with the flour and shape into tiny balls. When the soup has cooked for 15 minutes, remove the bay leaf and parsley. Add the cleaned, cooked shrimp, the cream and the Tabasco. Drop in the butter-flour balls and cook over low heat, uncovered, stirring frequently until the soup thickens. Serves 8.

MENU

Cajun Shrimp Bisque
Warm Croissants
Pecan Pie

Mulligatawny

By origin this flavorful chicken soup is Indian but it has been popularized and changed considerably by the British. The name is derived from an Indian word meaning "pepper water," and the dish is well seasoned with exotic spices from the East. This is one version.

**1 frying chicken, about 3 pounds, cut up,
washed and dried
1 medium-sized onion stuck with 4 cloves
2 carrots, scraped and sliced thickly
1 stalk celery, sliced thickly
6 cups chicken broth or water
salt, pepper to taste
1/4 cup butter or margarine
1 large onion, peeled and sliced thinly
2 tablespoons turmeric powder
1 teaspoon ground coriander
1 teaspoon cayenne pepper
1 garlic clove, crushed
1/3 cup all-purpose flour
1½ cups grated coconut, preferably unsweetened
hot cooked rice (about 2 cups)
1 large lemon, sliced**

Put the chicken in a large kettle. Add the onion with the cloves, the carrots, celery, chicken broth, salt and pepper and bring to a boil. Lower the heat and cook slowly, covered, for 30 minutes, or until the chicken is tender. Take out the chicken pieces and remove the meat from the bones. Cut the meat into bite-sized pieces and discard the skin and bones.

Strain and reserve the broth. Melt the butter in a large kettle. Add the onion and sauté over low heat until tender. Add the turmeric powder, coriander, cayenne and garlic and cook slowly 1 minute. Stir in the flour and mix well. Gradually add the strained broth and then the coconut, and cook slowly, stirring, for 10 minutes. Add the cooked chicken pieces and leave on the stove just long enough to heat them. Serve in wide bowls. Put the hot cooked rice in a bowl and the lemon slices on a plate, and pass them to each person to be added to the soup as garnishes. Serves 6.

MENU

Mulligatawny
Chapati or Whole Wheat Bread
Fresh Fruit Macédoine

Oriental Friendship Soup

In the Orient a fascinating variety of one-dish meals, cooked and served at the table, are called friendship dishes. The flavorful combination of typical Oriental foods can be prepared in the kitchen beforehand or, if desired, at the table. For a utensil use a large skillet, electric frying pan, a chimneyed oriental cooker or a kettle. Such a soup is marvelous for an informal supper.

1 tablespoon cornstarch
4 cups beef bouillon
1-2 tablespoons soy sauce
4 green onions, with 2 inches of tops, sliced
1 large onion, peeled and thinly sliced
peanut or vegetable oil
1½ pounds lean sirloin beef,
cut into paper thin slices
1 cup chopped celery
10 ounces fresh spinach leaves, washed,
trimmed and torn into small pieces

pepper to taste
1 can (1 pound) chow mein vegetables
2 cups very fine egg noodles, cooked and drained

In a large bowl combine the cornstarch with the bouillon and soy sauce, the exact amount depending on the desired flavor and type of brand. (Some kinds are stronger than others.) Set aside. Put the onions in the selected cooking utensil. Add 3 tablespoons peanut oil and heat. Sauté until the onions are limp. Push aside and add more oil and several slices of beef. Brown on both sides. Continue to add oil, as needed, and more beef slices, until all are browned. Add the celery, spinach and cornstarch-bouillon mixture. Mix well and season with pepper. Cook over medium heat, covered, for 10 minutes. Add the chow mein vegetables and cooked and drained noodles and cook about 5 minutes longer, until the ingredients are just tender. The vegetables should not be over-cooked. Serve from the cooking utensil, if desired, and ladle into large bowls. Serves 6.

MENU

Oriental Friendship Soup
Mixed Crackers
Mandarin Orange Sections
Almond Cookies

Salmon-Mushroom Bisque Smetana

This rich and delectable soup, flavored with *smetana*, the Russian word for sour cream, is especially suitable for a light luncheon.

1 pound fresh whole mushrooms
2 cans (1 pound each) red salmon
1 cup sliced green onions, with tops
1/4 cup butter or margarine
1/4 cup all-purpose flour

2 cups light cream or milk
1/4 teaspoon dried marjoram
1/2 teaspoon paprika
salt, pepper to taste
2 cups sour cream, at room temperature
2 tablespoons chopped fresh dill or parsley

Clean the mushrooms by rinsing quickly or wiping with a wet paper towel to remove any dirt. Cut off any tough stem ends. Wipe dry and cut into halves lengthwise. Drain and flake the salmon, reserving the liquid. Remove and discard any bones. Put the liquid in a large measuring cup and add enough water to make 2 cups. Sauté the green onions in the butter in a large kettle over low heat until tender. Mix in the flour and cook, stirring, about 1 minute. Gradually add the salmon liquid, and cook slowly, stirring, until thickened and smooth. Gradually add the cream or milk and continue to cook slowly. Add the marjoram, paprika, salt and pepper and cook until the sauce is thickened and smooth. Add the mushrooms and salmon and cook slowly, covered, for 10 minutes. Stir in the sour cream and dill; leave on the stove just long enough to heat through. Serves 8.

Note: If the dish is prepared beforehand, add the sour cream and dill just before serving.

MENU

Salmon-Mushroom Bisque Smetana
Hot Popovers
Bibb Lettuce Salad
Pineapple Bavarian Cream

Pasta and Fagioli

A favorite soup in the Tuscany region of Italy features pasta and white beans. In fact, so many of their dishes are made with the fat and tender white beans that the Tuscans are called "bean eaters" or *mangiafagioli* by other Italians. An economical dish with a delightful taste, this soup is good for a buffet party.

2 cups dried white beans
2 cups diced cooked ham, including some fat
1/4 cup olive or vegetable oil
2 large onions, peeled and chopped
3-4 garlic cloves, minced
4 stalks celery with leaves, chopped
2 large tomatoes, peeled and chopped
salt, pepper to taste
2 cups pasta (elbow macaroni, broken spaghetti,
cut-up linguine)
1/2 cup chopped fresh parsley
grated Parmesan cheese, preferably freshly grated

Pick over the beans and put in a large saucepan with cold water to cover. Bring to a boil; boil for 2 minutes. Remove from the heat and leave for 1 hour. When the beans are almost done, put the ham, oil, onions and garlic in a large pan and sauté them for 5 minutes. When the beans are ready, add them to the sautéed mixture, along with the celery, tomatoes, salt and pepper, and bring to a boil. Lower the heat and cook slowly, covered, about 1½ hours or until the beans are tender. Add more water while cooking, if needed. Uncover and bring the soup to a boil. Add the pasta and cook about 12 minutes, or until the pasta is tender. Stir in the parsley. Serve with grated Parmesan cheese sprinkled over each portion. Serves 12 to 14.

MENU

Pasta and Fagioli
Raw Spinach and Mushroom Salad
Bread Sticks
Biscuit Tortoni

Cotriade of Brittany

France's northern province of Brittany has been greatly influenced by the sea that surrounds three-quarters of it. Quite naturally there is an abundance of seafood to draw upon, and many superb dishes are made with it. *Cotriade*, often called the Breton *bouillabaisse*, is made with an assortment of the day's catch and flavored with onions and pungent herbs. It is a good luncheon or supper specialty.

3 pounds mixed fish, cleaned*
2 large onions, peeled and thinly sliced
1 large garlic clove, minced
3 tablespoons butter or margarine
6 medium-sized potatoes, pared and quartered
10 cups water
2 bay leaves
1 teaspoon dried thyme
4 parsley sprigs
1/2 teaspoon dried rosemary
salt, pepper to taste
slices of crusty French bread

Cut the fish into chunks or slices of equal size. Sauté the onions and garlic in the butter in a large kettle. Add the potatoes, water, bay leaves, thyme, parsley, rosemary, salt and pepper and bring to a boil. Add the prepared fish and lower the heat to moderate. Cook, covered, about 20 minutes, or until the fish are just tender and the potatoes are cooked. Ladle the broth over slices of bread in wide soup plates, and serve the potatoes and fish separately on a platter. Serves 6. *Halibut, haddock, sea bass, flounder, cod, mullet and/or mackerel are all suitable.

MENU

Cotriade of Brittany
Mixed Green Salad
Cheese Plate with French Bread

Canadian Pea Soup with Bacon

French Canadian cookery, a fascinating medley of Old and New World cuisines, boasts many substantial dishes. But the staff of life in the northeastern provinces has long been a hearty pea soup made with either dried yellow or green peas. This one, which includes Canadian bacon, is a good winter luncheon or supper dish.

1 pound green split peas
1/3 cup diced salt pork or bacon
2 medium-sized onions, peeled and chopped
2 carrots, scraped and diced
8 cups water
2 small bay leaves
6 parsley sprigs
1/2 teaspoon celery seed
1/8 teaspoon dry mustard
salt, pepper to taste
1/2 pound Canadian bacon, sliced
cheese croutons (recipe follows)

Wash and drain the peas. Combine the pork, onions and carrots in a large kettle and sauté them over low heat for 10 minutes. Add the water, peas, bay leaves, parsley, celery seed, mustard, salt and pepper and bring to a boil. Boil, uncovered, for 2 minutes. Remove from the stove and let stand, covered, for 1 hour. Return to the stove and simmer, covered, for about 1½ hours, or until the peas are tender. Remove from the stove. Put through a sieve or whirl in a blender to purée. Slice the bacon thinly and cut each slice in half. Sauté over low heat in a skillet for 5 minutes. Reheat the soup over a low flame and add the bacon to it. Serve with cheese croutons. Serves 6.

Cheese Croutons

Trim the crusts from 4 slices of day-old bread and butter each on both sides. Cut into 1/4-inch cubes. Sprinkle with grated Parmesan cheese and brown in a preheated moderate oven (350°F.).

MENU

Canadian Pea Soup with Bacon
Sliced Cucumber-Tomato Salad
Blueberry Crisp or Pie

Pistou

One of the world's best soups, originally from Italy, now belongs to France's lovely Provence. Very similar to minestrone, its name derives from a spicy sauce or *pistou*, made with crushed garlic, olive oil, grated cheese and fresh basil. It is added to the soup at the end of the cooking. The soup is best when made in France in early spring with small fresh white beans, but this version is prepared with dried white beans.

3 tablespoons butter or olive oil
1 cup diced onion
2 leeks, white parts only, cleaned and sliced
2 large tomatoes, peeled and chopped
12 cups water
salt, pepper to taste
2 cups diced raw potatoes
2 cups cut-up green beans
2 unpeeled zucchini (about 3/4 pound), washed and diced
1 can (1 pound) *cannellini* or navy beans, drained
1/2 cup broken spaghettini or vermicelli
3-4 garlic cloves, crushed or minced
1/2 cup chopped fresh sweet basil or
1½ tablespoons dried basil
1/2 cup freshly grated Parmesan cheese
4 tablespoons olive oil

Heat the butter or oil in a large kettle. Add the onion and leeks and sauté them over low heat until tender. Add the tomatoes and cook about 3 minutes, until mushy. Pour in the water and bring to a boil. Season with salt and pepper. Stir in the potatoes and green beans. Lower the heat and simmer, uncovered, for 15 minutes. Add the zucchini, beans and spaghettini and cook another 15 minutes, or until the vegetables are tender. While the soup is cooking, prepare the sauce. In a mortar with a pestle (or bowl with a wooden spoon), pound the garlic and basil to form a paste. Stir in the cheese. Add the oil, 1 tablespoon at a time, and beat to make a thick paste. Just before serving add 2 cups of the hot soup to the paste. Gradually stir into the hot soup and serve at once. Pass grated cheese with it. Serves 12.

MENU

Pistou
Bread Sticks
Strawberry Tarts

Cape Cod Corn-Clam Chowder

Early settlers in New England created several variations of a thick soup that they called chowder. The name was taken from a large French kettle, a *chaudière*, used by fishermen in Brittany. This chowder combines favorite foods of Cape Cod to make a good winter luncheon or supper dish.

1/4 cup diced salt pork or bacon
2 medium-sized onions, peeled and chopped
2½ cups diced potatoes
2 cans (8 ounces each) minced clams, undrained
4 cups clam juice
2 cups frozen whole-kernel corn
1 teaspoon celery salt
salt, pepper to taste
4 cups rich milk
2 tablespoons butter or margarine
2 tablespoons chopped fresh parsley

Combine the pork and onions in a large kettle. Sauté over low heat until the onions are tender. Add the potatoes, clams, clam juice, corn, celery salt, salt and pepper and bring to a boil. Lower the heat and cook slowly, covered, about 12 minutes or until the potatoes are tender. Add the milk, butter and parsley, and leave on the stove long enough to heat through. Serves 4 to 6.

Note: Canned corn can be used instead of the frozen corn; add it with the milk, butter and parsley.

MENU

Cape Cod Corn-Clam Chowder
Cole Slaw
Warm Parker House Rolls
Boston Cream Pie

Scotch Cock-a-Leekie

This famous Scotch soup, featuring chicken and leeks, obtained its name probably because it was once made with a cockerel or young rooster. Possibly this was in the days when cock fighting was a popular sport and the defeated bird ended up in the soup pot. Some recipes call for the addition of prunes. This one includes barley, a favorite Scotch food.

1 stewing chicken, about 5 pounds, washed and dried
20 cups water
12 leeks, white parts and 2 inches of green stems,
washed and cut into 1/4-inch lengths
4 parsley sprigs
1 bay leaf
1/2 teaspoon dried thyme
salt, pepper to taste
1/2 cup pearl barley
2 tablespoons chopped fresh parsley

Put the chicken in a large kettle and add the water. Bring to a boil. Use a skimmer or spoon to remove any scum that has risen to the surface. Add all the remaining ingredients except the chopped fresh parsley, and lower the heat. Cook

slowly, partially covered, until the chicken is tender, about
2½ hours. Remove the chicken to a large plate or platter, and
when slightly cooled, remove and discard the skin. Bone the
chicken and cut into bite-sized pieces. Remove and discard
the parsley sprigs and bay leaf from the liquid. Take off
any scum from the surface of the liquid and return the
chicken to the kettle. Put the soup back on the stove long
enough to heat through. Serve garnished with the chopped
parsley. Serves 10.

MENU

Scotch Cock-a-Leekie
Oatmeal Bread
Stewed Fruit Compote

Dutch Vermicelli-Veal Meatball Soup

This soup from Holland combines three favorite Dutch
foods, including meatballs, *balletjes*. The Dutch relish this
soup during their long cold winters as it is nourishing and
hearty.

2 pounds ground veal
2 eggs
4 teaspoons curry powder
salt, pepper to taste
4 slices white bread, without crusts
milk
2 large onions, peeled and chopped
2 large carrots, scraped and chopped
2 leeks, white parts only, cleaned and sliced
2 large celery stalks, chopped
1/4 cup butter or margarine
2 tablespoons vegetable oil
12 cups beef bouillon
or
12 cups of water and 12 bouillon cubes

1/2 teaspoon dried marjoram
3 cups broken vermicelli
1/2 cup chopped fresh parsley

Combine the veal, eggs, curry powder, salt and pepper in a large bowl and mix well. Soak the bread in milk to cover. Squeeze dry and break into tiny pieces. Add to the veal-egg combination and mix well again. Shape into 1½-inch balls and set aside. Sauté the onions, carrots, leeks and celery in the butter or margarine and oil in a large kettle over low heat for 10 minutes. Add the bouillon and marjoram and season with salt and pepper. Bring to a boil. Lower the heat and cook slowly, covered, for 30 minutes. Add the meatballs and cook about another 20 minutes, or until they are tender. Meanwhile, cook the vermicelli in boiling water until just tender; drain. When the meatballs are cooked, add the vermicelli. Remove from the heat and serve garnished with the parsley. Serves 10.

Note: For a thinner soup add more bouillon.

MENU

Dutch Vermicelli-Veal Meatball Soup
Hearts of Lettuce Salad
Strawberry Meringues

Greek Island Fish Soup with Sea Shells

Some of the world's earliest fish soups were created by fishermen from the Grecian Islands. This version is further enhanced by the addition of pasta sea shells to the other typically Greek ingredients.

2 large onions, peeled and chopped
2-3 garlic cloves, crushed
6 tablespoons olive or vegetable oil
3/4 cup tomato paste
8 cups vegetable bouillon or water

**1½ teaspoons dried oregano or marjoram
2 small bay leaves
salt, pepper to taste
2 pounds white fleshed fish fillets (flounder, cod, halibut),
cut into bite-sized pieces
1 cup pasta sea shells
1/3 cup chopped fresh parsley
or 2 tablespoons chopped fresh dill**

Sauté the onions and garlic in the oil in a large kettle over low heat for 5 minutes. Add the tomato paste, bouillon or water, oregano, bay leaves, salt and pepper, and bring to a boil. Lower the heat and add the fish. Cook slowly, covered, until the fish is just fork tender, about 12 minutes. Add the sea shells and cook over medium heat, uncovered, until just tender, about 10 minutes. Remove from the heat. Take out and discard the bay leaves. Stir in the parsley. Serves 6 to 8.
Note: More liquid may be added during the cooking to make a thinner soup.

MENU

***Greek Island Fish Soup with Sea Shells
Sliced Cucumbers
Crisp Crackers
Nut-Honey Covered Cake***

Petite Marmite

One of the great classic French soups, *petite marmite*, which means literally "small kettle," takes its name from the pot, or *marmite*, in which it is traditionally cooked and served. Some of the best preparations are found in French country restaurants. This is one of many good versions. It is a good dish for an informal sit-down dinner.

**2 medium-sized onions, peeled and sliced
2 tablespoons butter or vegetable oil**

2 pounds chuck or other beef in one piece
1 pound beef soup bones
2 pounds chicken wings
12 cups beef bouillon or water
2 bay leaves
4 whole cloves
4 parsley sprigs
1/2 teaspoon dried thyme
6 peppercorns, bruised
salt to taste
3 medium-sized leeks, white parts only, cleaned and sliced
4 carrots, scraped and cut into 1-inch pieces
4 medium-sized white turnips, peeled and quartered
3 cups cut-up frozen green beans
1 loaf French bread, sliced thickly and toasted
grated Parmesan cheese, preferably freshly grated

Sauté the onions in the butter in a large kettle over low heat until tender. Add the beef, beef bones, chicken wings, bouillon, bay leaves, cloves, parsley sprigs, thyme, peppercorns and salt, and bring slowly to a full simmer. Remove any scum. Cook very slowly, covered, for 2½ hours, occasionally removing any scum that has risen to the top. Add the leeks, carrots and turnips, and continue to cook slowly about another 30 minutes, or until the meat and vegetables are tender. Add the green beans 10 minutes before the cooking is finished. Remove the kettle from the stove. Take out and discard the bay leaves, cloves, parsley and peppercorns. Take out the beef, soup bones and chicken wings. Keep the broth and vegetables warm over low heat. Cut the beef into slices. Remove any meat from the beef bones and chicken wings. To serve, put some of the beef, chicken and warm vegetables into individual soup plates. Cover with some of the hot broth. Serve with toasted French bread and grated cheese. Serves 6.

MENU

Petite Marmite
French Pastry

Polish Kielbasi-Lentil Zupa

The art of making sausages is very ancient; some of the best have been created by the Poles. In their country the general term for all sausages is *kielbasi*. In America this generally refers to the highly seasoned meat called Polish sausage. This is a good, hearty supper dish.

1 ham bone (optional)
2 medium-sized onions, peeled and chopped
2 carrots, scraped and chopped
2 stalks celery, cleaned and chopped
8 cups water
2 cups lentils, washed and drained
2 small bay leaves
salt, pepper to taste
1½ pounds *kielbasi* or Polish sausage
2 tablespoons wine vinegar

If a ham bone is to be included in the soup, cut some fat from it and render the fat in a large kettle. Otherwise, use 2 tablespoons of any other kind of fat and heat it in a kettle. Add the onions, carrots and celery and sauté over low heat for 5 minutes. Add the ham bone, water, lentils, bay leaves, salt and pepper, and bring to a boil. Lower the heat and simmer until the lentils are just tender, about 30 minutes. Cut the sausage into 1-inch slices and add to the soup. Cook another 15 minutes. Add the vinegar and stir well. Remove and discard the ham bone and bay leaves. Serves 10.

MENU

Polish Kielbasi-Lentil Zupa
Mixed Green Salad
Rye Bread
Plum Dumplings or Cake

Minestrone Alla Romano

The best known of the great repertoire of Italian soups outside the country is the thick vegetable soup called minestrone. The ingredients vary greatly but usually there are a number of dried and fresh vegetables and either rice or pasta. The name derives from the Latin for "hand out." Long ago monks kept pots of the soup on their monastery stoves to hand out to hungry wayfarers.

3 thin slices bacon, chopped
1 tablespoon olive or vegetable oil
1 large onion, peeled and chopped
3 leeks, white parts only, cleaned and thinly sliced
1-2 garlic cloves, crushed
1 large carrot, scraped and diced
2 cups chopped green cabbage
2 unpeeled zucchini (about 1/2 pound each), sliced
1 can (1 pound) tomatoes, undrained and chopped
1½ cups diced raw potatoes
8 cups beef bouillon or water
salt, pepper to taste
1 can (1 pound) white or kidney beans, drained
1 cup small pasta or broken up spaghetti
grated Parmesan cheese, preferably freshly grated

Combine the bacon, oil, onion, leeks and garlic in a large kettle and sauté the vegetables over low heat for 5 minutes. Add the carrot and cabbage and sauté for another 5 minutes. Add the zucchini, tomatoes, potatoes and bouillon or water and bring to a boil. Season with salt and pepper. Lower the heat and cook slowly, covered, until the ingredients are just tender, about 30 minutes. Add the beans and pasta and cook over moderate heat about 15 minutes longer, or until the pasta is tender. Serve with grated Parmesan cheese. Serves 10.

MENU

Minestrone Alla Romano
Bread Sticks
Bel Paese Cheese and Fresh Grapes

New Orleans Chicken and Okra Gumbo

Favorite fare in Louisiana includes the native Creole gumbos made with seafood, poultry or meat, and vegetables, as well as spicy seasonings. The word *gumbo* is taken from the Bantu for okra, and the dish is traditionally thickened with this vegetable, or with *filé* powder, which is made from ground dried sassafras leaves. It is a good dish for a summer luncheon served outdoors.

1 frying chicken, about 3 pounds, cut up
1 medium-sized onion, peeled and chopped
1 cup diced smoked ham
2 tablespoons lard or bacon drippings
2 cans (1 pound each) tomatoes, undrained
2 packages (10 ounces each) sliced frozen okra, defrosted
6 cups boiling water
1 bay leaf
4 sprigs parsley
1/4 teaspoon dried thyme
1 pod of red pepper, seeded, or 1/8 teaspoon cayenne
1 teaspoon *filé* powder (optional)
3 cups cooked rice

Cut the chicken legs, wings and breasts into a total of 12 pieces. Wash and wipe dry. Sauté the onion and ham in the lard in a kettle over low heat until the onion is tender. Add the chicken and fry until golden. Mix in the tomatoes and cook 1 minute, breaking them with a spoon. Add the remaining ingredients, except the *filé* powder and rice, and bring to a boil. Lower the heat and simmer, covered, for 1 hour. Remove the cover and continue to cook about 30 minutes longer, or until the chicken and okra are tender. Stir in the *filé* powder just before removing from the heat. Do not allow the soup to boil after adding the *filé* powder. Pour 1/2 cup of rice into each of 6 large soup plates, and ladle the gumbo over it. Serves 6.

MENU

New Orleans Chicken and Okra Gumbo
Romaine Lettuce Salad
French Bread
Strawberry Soufflé

Soupe de Poissons

In southern France there are two great soups which often cause culinary confusion as both names, *soupe aux poissons* and *soupe de poissons*, are used interchangeably on menus. Recipes for them are also not clear; but each is a marvelous combination of flavors. This version, from the colorful seaport of Marseilles, is made with pasta.

1 large onion, peeled and finely chopped
2 leeks, white parts only, cleaned and thinly sliced
1/3 cup olive or vegetable oil
2 garlic cloves, crushed
3 medium-sized tomatoes, peeled and chopped
1 bay leaf
1 small piece orange rind
1 tablespoon chopped fresh parsley
8 cups water
2 pounds mixed cleaned fish and shellfish (small lobster, crab, red snapper, haddock, sea bass, cod, rockfish, mackerel), cut into large pieces of equal size
1/2 pound vermicelli, broken into 1-inch pieces
salt, pepper to taste
pinch of saffron (optional)

Sauté the onion and leeks in the oil in a large kettle over low heat until tender. Add the garlic, tomatoes, bay leaf, orange rind, parsley and water. Bring to a boil. Add the fish and shellfish and lower the heat. Cook, uncovered, until the seafood is tender, about 10 minutes. Carefully remove the seafood to a platter and keep warm. Strain the liquid. Reheat and add the vermicelli, salt, pepper and saffron. Cook over high heat about 5 minutes or until the vermicelli is just tender. To serve, put portions of the seafood in wide soup plates and ladle the broth and vermicelli over it. Serves 6.

· MENU

Soupe de Poissons
French Bread
Raspberry Sherbet

Ham and Bean Potage Indienne

One of the world's oldest seasonings is a blend of spices called curry powder. Native to India, the mixture may consist of a few spices, such as turmeric, coriander, red or cayenne pepper, or cumin seed, or may include a larger number. Some combinations are hotter than others. A mixture of spices gives this soup the taste of curry.

2 cups dried white beans, washed and drained
5 cups water
1 large onion, peeled and chopped
1 garlic clove, crushed
2 tablespoons peanut or vegetable oil
2 teaspoons turmeric powder
1/2 teaspoon cayenne
1/2 teaspoon ground coriander
1/2 teaspoon ground cloves
salt, pepper to taste
1 can (1 pound) tomatoes
2 cups plain yogurt
3 cups chopped cooked ham

Put the beans and water in a large kettle. Boil, uncovered, for 2 minutes. Remove from the heat and let stand, covered, for 1 hour. When the beans are nearly done, sauté the onion and garlic in the oil in a skillet over low heat until tender. Add the turmeric, cayenne, coriander, cloves, salt and pepper and cook for 1 minute. Remove from the heat and add to the cooked beans. Add the tomatoes. Bring the mixture to a boil. Lower the heat and cook slowly, covered, until the beans are tender, about 1 hour. Stir in the yogurt and ham and leave on the stove just long enough to heat through. Serves 6 to 8.

MENU

Ham and Bean Potage Indienne
Whole Wheat Bread
Lemon Ice Cream Pie

Riviera Rice-Veal Potage

This soup is a flavorful medley of ingredients commonly used in the cookery of the sun-kissed strip of southern France called the Riviera. The soup is easy and economical to prepare, and will lend itself to an attractive informal buffet.

1 cup chopped onion
1-2 garlic cloves, crushed
2 tablespoons butter or olive oil
1½ pounds ground veal
1 can (1 pound, 12 ounces) tomatoes
1/2 teaspoon dried oregano
1/2 teaspoon dried rosemary
salt, pepper to taste
4-6 cups tomato juice
1 cup uncooked rice
3 cups cut-up frozen green beans
1/3 cup chopped fresh parsley

Sauté the onion and garlic in the butter in a large kettle over low heat until tender. Add the veal; cook, mincing with a fork, until the redness disappears. Add the tomatoes, oregano, rosemary, salt and pepper, and cook slowly, covered, for 30 minutes. Add the tomato juice, varying the exact amount to the desired thickness of the soup, and the rice. Cook slowly, covered, for 10 minutes. Add the green beans. Continue to cook about 10 minutes longer, or until the rice and green beans are tender. Stir in the parsley. Remove from the heat and serve. Serves 10 to 12.

Note: If this soup is prepared beforehand, do not add the green beans until after it is reheated.

MENU

Riviera Rice-Veal Potage
Crisp Crackers
Orange Sherbet Coupes

Texas Kidney Bean-Chili Soup

A good dish for an informal dinner.

2 cups dried red kidney beans, washed and drained
6 cups water
1 large bay leaf
4 sprigs parsley
salt, pepper to taste
2 medium-sized onions, peeled and chopped
2 garlic cloves, crushed
2 tablespoons vegetable oil
1-2 teaspoons chili powder
2 pounds lean ground beef
4 cups tomato juice
2 cups chopped green pepper

Put the beans in a large kettle and add the water, bay leaf, parsley, salt and pepper. Bring to a boil; boil for 2 minutes. Remove from the stove and let stand for 1 hour. Return to the stove and simmer, covered, for 1 hour. While the beans are cooking, sauté the onions and garlic in the oil in a skillet over low heat until tender. Stir in the chili powder and cook several seconds. Push the onions aside and add the beef. Cook slowly, mincing with a fork, until the redness disappears. Remove from the stove and set aside. After the beans have cooked for 1 hour, add the onion-beef mixture and the tomato juice. Mix well and continue to simmer another 30 minutes or until the beans are tender. Add the chopped pepper 5 minutes before the cooking is finished. Correct the seasoning and remove from the heat. Take out and discard the parsley sprigs and bay leaf. Serves 6.

Note: If the dish is prepared beforehand, add the green peppers after it is reheated.

MENU

Texas Kidney Bean-Chili Soup
Avocado-Lettuce Salad
Warm Corn Bread
Vanilla Ice Cream with Pineapple Sauce

Catalan Ouillade

The French area of Catalan and the nearby Spanish region of Catalonia have many similar dishes that rely heavily on garlic and olive oil. This soup, one of the best-known specialties, takes its name from the earthenware dishes, *ouilles*, in which it is traditionally cooked. Although the ingredients vary, beans and cabbage are essential. They are cooked separately, but timed to be ready simultaneously.

1 cup dried white beans, washed and drained
3 slices thick bacon, chopped
2 tablespoons olive or vegetable oil
1 large onion, peeled and chopped
1 carrot, scraped and diced
3 garlic cloves, crushed
3½ cups shredded green cabbage

1/2 teaspoon dried thyme
2 tablespoons chopped fresh parsley
salt, pepper to taste
3 medium-sized potatoes, pared and quartered
1 small piece salt pork
1 tablespoon chopped fresh herbs (rosemary, tarragon,
oregano) or 1/2 teaspoon dried herbs

Put the beans in an earthenware pot or a kettle and cover with water. Bring to a boil. Cover and cook 2 minutes. Remove from the heat and let stand for 1 hour. Meanwhile, prepare the ingredients for the cabbage mixture, which will be put on the stove at the same time as the bean mixture. For the cabbage mixture, combine the bacon, oil, onion, carrot and 2 cloves of garlic in an earthenware pot or kettle. Sauté them for 5 minutes. Add 4 cups of water, the shredded cabbage, thyme, parsley, salt and pepper, and bring to a boil. Turn the heat as low as possible and cook slowly, tightly covered, for 1½ hours. Add the potatoes after the mixture has cooked for 1 hour.

Drain the beans after soaking for 1 hour; cover with 2 cups of water. Add the remaining garlic clove, salt pork and herbs and season with salt and pepper. Bring to a boil. Lower the heat and cook very slowly about 1½ hours, or until just tender. Add more water while cooking, if needed. Combine with the cabbage mixture just before serving. Serves 6.

MENU

Catalan Ouillade
Hot Garlic Bread
Pears with Raspberry Purée

German Lentil-Frankfurter Eintopf

In Germany a typical one-dish meal is an *Eintopf*, a nourishing soup or stew that is a great family favorite and a featured specialty at inns and restaurants. Traditionally it is enjoyed amid an informal and gay atmosphere with foaming steins of beer. This is a good dish for a buffet or late evening party.

**6 slices thin bacon, chopped
2 medium-sized onions, peeled and chopped
2 carrots, scraped and diced
2 stalks celery, cleaned and diced
2 cups dried lentils, washed and drained
8 cups water
1/2 teaspoon dried thyme
salt, pepper to taste
2 cans (8 ounces each) tomato sauce
8 frankfurters, cut into 1-inch slices
3 tablespoons cider vinegar
1/4 cup chopped fresh parsley**

Put the bacon, onions, carrots and celery in a large kettle and sauté over low heat for 10 minutes. Add the lentils, water, thyme, salt and pepper, and mix well. Bring to a boil. Lower the heat and simmer, covered, for 1 hour. Add the tomato sauce and frankfurters and cook another 15 minutes, or until the lentils are tender but not mushy. Stir in the vinegar and parsley and check the seasoning. Serves 12 to 14.

MENU

*German Lentil-Frankfurter Eintopf
Mixed Green Salad
Rye Bread
Apple Kuchen*

Mexican Rice-Chicken Sopa

This soup is flavored with *recaudo*, a typical Mexican sauce that is made with onions, garlic, green chilies and tomatoes. Avocados add further appeal.

2 medium-sized onions, peeled and chopped
2 garlic cloves, crushed
3 tablespoons peanut or vegetable oil
2 canned green chilies, rinsed, seeded and minced
3 large tomatoes, peeled and chopped
1-2 teaspoons chili powder (optional)
1 can (1 pound) tomatoes, undrained
2½ pounds (about) cut-up chicken pieces,
washed and dried
12 cups chicken broth or water
1/2 teaspoon dried oregano
salt, pepper to taste
1 cup uncooked rice
2 cans (12 ounces each) whole kernel corn
2 medium-sized ripe avocados, peeled, pitted and cubed
1/3 cup chopped fresh coriander or parsley

Sauté the onions and garlic in the oil in a large kettle over low heat until tender. Add the chilies, chopped fresh tomatoes and chili powder and sauté 3 minutes. Then add the canned tomatoes, chicken pieces, broth, oregano, salt and pepper and bring to a boil. Lower the heat and cook slowly, covered, for 30 minutes. Add the rice and continue to cook slowly for another 30 minutes, or until the chicken and rice are tender. Add the corn and avocado cubes 10 minutes before the cooking is finished. Remove from the heat and take out the chicken pieces. Cut the chicken from the bones and return to the soup. Discard the skin and bones. Stir in the coriander or parsley. Reheat, if necessary. Serves 8.
Note: If the soup is prepared beforehand, do not add the corn, avocados and coriander until just before serving.

MENU

Mexican Rice-Chicken Sopa
Warm Tortillas
Coconut Cake or Pie

Danish Gule Aerter

A thick yellow pea soup called *gule aerter* has long been an important winter dish in Denmark. Each housewife has her own favorite recipe for the family soup. Some prefer to sieve the peas. Others do not. Sausages are included in several variations but not in all of them. Traditionally, however, the soup is prepared in ample supply and served with dark rye bread, mustard, beer and ice cold *schnapps* (a strong clear alcoholic drink).

2 cups (1 pound) yellow split peas, washed and drained
1½-2 pounds lean bacon or smoked pork in one piece
6-8 cups water
3 carrots, scraped
1 celeriac, washed, peeled and quartered (optional)
4 medium-sized leeks, white parts only, cleaned and sliced
2 medium-sized onions, peeled and cut into halves
1/2 teaspoon dried thyme
salt, pepper to taste
1 pound pork sausage links, cooked and drained

Soak the peas in cold water according to package directions. Cook slowly, covered, in 6 cups of water in a large saucepan until soft, about 1½ hours. Put the bacon, carrots, celeriac, leeks, onions, thyme, salt and pepper in another large saucepan or kettle and cover with water. Cook slowly, covered, about 30 minutes, or until the vegetables and bacon are tender. Take out the bacon; slice and keep warm. Take out the vegetables and cut up into smaller pieces, if desired. Add to the cooked peas with as much of the vegetable broth as needed for desired consistency. Reheat, if necessary. Ladle the soup into wide soup plates and pass the sliced bacon and sausages separately. Serves 6 to 8.

MENU

Danish Gule Aerter
Rye Bread
Spice Cake

Belgian Chicken Waterzooi

One of the great Flemish creations of Belgium is a thick soup, *Waterzooi*, made with either fish or chicken cooked in a rich lemon-flavored broth. This version also includes frozen peas, which is not a typical ingredient.

2 medium-sized onions, peeled and chopped
2 medium-sized leeks, white parts only, cleaned and sliced
3 stalks celery, cleaned and chopped
2 carrots, scraped and chopped
11 tablespoons (about) butter or margarine
4½-5 pounds broiler-fryer chickens cut in pieces
(or equivalent amount of chicken legs and thighs),
washed and dried
6 cups chicken broth or bouillon
1 bay leaf
4 whole cloves
1/2 teaspoon dried thyme
3 parsley sprigs
6 peppercorns
1½-2 teaspoons salt
1/4 cup flour
2 cups frozen green peas, cooked and drained
2 egg yolks
juice of 1 large lemon
1 large lemon, sliced
1/4 cup chopped fresh parsley

Sauté the onions, leeks, celery and carrots in 4 tablespoons of butter in a large kettle over low heat for 5 minutes. Remove with a slotted spoon to a plate. Melt 4 tablespoons of butter in the kettle and sauté the chicken pieces on both sides in it. Sauté a few pieces at a time. Add more butter, if needed. Return the sautéed vegetables and all the chicken pieces to the kettle. Add the broth, bay leaf, cloves, thyme, parsley sprigs, peppercorns and salt. Bring to a boil. Lower the heat and cook slowly, covered, about 30 minutes, or until the chicken is tender. Remove the kettle from the stove and take out the chicken pieces. Keep warm. Strain the broth into another kettle and leave over low heat. Melt 3 tablespoons of butter in a saucepan. Stir in the flour. Gradually add 2 cups of the hot broth, stirring constantly, and cook slowly until thick and smooth. Add the cooked peas. Beat the egg yolks slightly with the lemon juice, and add a little of the hot broth. Mix well and return to the soup. Cook over low heat, stirring, until thickened and smooth. Correct the seasonings. To serve, pour the broth and peas over the warm chicken pieces. Garnish with the lemon slices and chopped parsley. Serves 8.

MENU

Belgian Chicken Waterzooi
Crusty White Bread
Warm Gingerbread

Bouillabaisse

One of the world's most famous soups, *bouillabaisse*, has been extolled by poets, writers and cooks for centuries. Like any renowned dish there are many versions of it but the true *bouillabaisse* is generally conceded to be that prepared in the colorful southern French port of Marseilles and nearby villages. The name is a combination of the word *"boil,"* or *bouille*, and the word *"let down,"* or *baisse*, and the cooking of the soup is exactly that. Essential ingredients are seafood, olive oil, garlic, tomatoes and seasonings of fennel, thyme, bay leaf and orange peel. There are many opinions about the kinds of seafood needed, but generally speaking, a good *bouillabaisse* should include a variety of crustaceans and fish. Outside the Mediterranean it is necessary to use substitutes for some of the native kinds. Suggestions inlcude lobsters, crabs; soft-fleshed fish such as sole, sea perch, flounder, red snapper and whiting; firm-fleshed fish such as cod, haddock, sea bass, rockfish and mackerel. Many cooks insist that eel is essential. The choice very often depends on the kinds of seafood that are available.

4 pounds mixed fish and shellfish
1/3 cup olive or vegetable oil
2 medium-sized onions, peeled and chopped
2-3 garlic cloves, crushed
3 large tomatoes, peeled, seeded and chopped
1 large bay leaf
1 large piece of fennel, chopped, or 1/2 teaspoon
fennel seeds
1 large piece of orange peel, diced
1 tablespoon chopped fresh parsley
1/4 teaspoon dried thyme
water
salt, pepper to taste
1/4 teaspoon whole or ground saffron
slices of plain or toasted French bread
***rouille* sauce (recipe below)**

Have the fish and shellfish cleaned and ready beforehand. Small ones can be left whole. Larger ones should be cut into similar-sized pieces. If lobsters or large crabs are to be used, cut them up. Separate the firmer-fleshed fish from the more delicate ones as the former should be added before the latter. Heat the oil in a large kettle. Add the onions and sauté until tender. Add the garlic, tomatoes, bay leaf, fennel, orange peel, parsley and thyme. Cook slowly, stirring, for 5 minutes. Place any crustaceans and firm-fleshed fish over the mixture and cook over fairly high heat for 5 minutes. Add the more delicate fish and boiling water to cover. Season with salt and pepper. Add the saffron. Bring the mixture to a boil. Lower the heat and cook slowly, covered, until the fish are just tender, about 10 minutes. To serve, ladle the broth over one or more pieces of crusty bread in a large soup plate. Serve the fish and shellfish on a separate platter. Pass the *rouille* sauce in a bowl. Serves 8.

Rouille Sauce

2-3 garlic cloves
2 hot red peppers, seeded

1/4 cup soft dry bread crumbs
1/4 cup olive oil
3/4-1 cup hot broth from the soup

Pound together the garlic and red peppers. Add the bread crumbs and pound again. Add the oil to make a thick paste and thin with the hot broth.

MENU

Bouillabaisse
Mixed Green Salad
Cold Lemon Soufflé

Viennese Chicken-Vegetable Pot

This nourishing and flavorful soup is a good family dish. Serve for a weekend dinner.

1 stewing or roasting chicken, about 4 pounds
salt, pepper to taste
2 large onions, peeled and sliced
2 tablespoons butter or margarine
1 tablespoon vegetable oil
12 cups water
bouquet garni **(3 sprigs parsley, 1 bay leaf, 1/4 teaspoon**
dried thyme)
1/2 pound fresh mushrooms, cleaned
2 cups frozen mixed vegetables
1 can (6 ounces) tomato paste
1/2 pound fine egg noodles, cooked and drained
1/4 teaspoon paprika

Wash the chicken and wipe dry. Sprinkle inside and out with salt and pepper. Sauté the sliced onions in the butter and oil in a large kettle over low heat until tender. Add the chicken and brown until golden on all sides, turning carefully with two large spoons. Add the water and *bouquet garni*; bring to a boil. Lower the heat and simmer, covered, for 1 hour, or until the chicken is tender. Remove from the heat and cool. Take the chicken meat from the bones and cut into bite-sized pieces. Discard the bones and skin. Strain the broth. Return it and the chicken pieces to the kettle. Add the mushrooms, vegetables and tomato paste to the chicken. Reheat and cook slowly, covered, for about 7 minutes, or until the vegetables are tender. Stir in the noodles and add the paprika. Serves 8.

MENU

Viennese Chicken-Vegetable Pot
Warm Poppy-Seed Rolls
Nut Torte

Creole Shrimp-Rice Potage

The spicy Creole cookery of Louisiana evolved as a result of a fascinating combination of French, Spanish and West Indian cuisines. Some Creole foods are of African or American Indian origin. Two favorite Creole foods, shrimp and rice, are used in this flavorful soup.

2 pounds raw unshelled shrimp
1 medium-sized lemon, sliced
1 bay leaf
1 teaspoon dried thyme
salt, pepper to taste
water
3 tablespoons bacon drippings or other fat
1 cup chopped onion
1/2 cup chopped celery
1/2 cup chopped green pepper
1 can (1 pound) tomatoes, undrained
6 cups chicken broth or bouillon
1/2 cup uncooked rice
Tabasco sauce to taste

Put the shrimp in a large kettle. Add the sliced lemon, bay leaf, 1/2 teaspoon of the thyme, salt, pepper and water to cover. Bring to a boil. Lower the heat and simmer, uncovered, about 5 minutes, or until the shrimp turn pink. (It will take longer if the shrimp are in a frozen block.) Remove from the stove and drain. Cool, peel and clean the shrimp.

Heat the bacon drippings in a large kettle. Add the onion, celery and green pepper and sauté over low heat for 10 minutes. Add the tomatoes and cook over low heat for 1 minute, breaking them with a spoon. Pour in the chicken broth and bring to a boil. Stir in the rice, the remaining 1/2 teaspoon of thyme and season with salt and pepper. Lower the heat and cook slowly, covered, about 20 minutes, or until the rice is tender. Add the shrimp and Tabasco and mix well. Leave on the stove long enough to heat the shrimp. Serves 8. *Note: This soup also can be made with 1 pound of cooked, peeled and cleaned shrimp. Add them at the end of the cooking.*

MENU

Creole Shrimp-Rice Potage
Warm Corn Muffins
Baked Bananas with Ice Cream

Sopa de Albondigas

Meatballs, *albondigas*, are great South American favorites, which are flavored in various ways. These are spicy and make a good supper dish.

1 pound lean ground beef
1 slice stale white bread
1 egg, beaten
1 garlic clove, crushed
2 tablespoons minced fresh parsley
salt, pepper to taste
1 medium-sized onion, peeled and chopped
1 tablespoon vegetable oil

1-2 teaspoons chili powder
1 can (1 pound) tomatoes, undrained
1 can (6 ounces) tomato paste
8 cups beef bouillon

Put the ground beef in a large bowl. Cover the slice of bread with water in another bowl. When soft, squeeze dry to release all the water and break into small pieces. Add the bread, egg, garlic, parsley, salt and pepper. Mix well until all ingredients are thoroughly combined. Shape into 3/4-inch balls and set aside. Sauté the onions in the oil in a large kettle over low heat until tender. Stir in the chili powder and cook several seconds. Add the tomatoes and break up with a spoon. Stir in the tomato paste and cook 1 minute. Add the bouillon and bring to a boil. Season with salt and pepper. Drop the meatballs into it. Lower the heat and simmer, covered, about 45 minutes, or until the meatballs are done. Serves 8.

MENU

Sopa de Albondigas
Lettuce-Avocado Salad
Warm Corn Bread
Crème Caramel

Russian Borscht

Russia's most famous soup, *borscht*, is based on beets, from which it gets its coloring. Sometimes it is a simple dish of beets, liquid and a few flavorings, but it can also be a rich soup laden with other vegetables and meats. This soup is traditionally served with sour cream. This *borscht* from the region of the Ukraine is a hearty one, good for a winter dinner.

8 medium-sized beets
1/2 cup vinegar
salt

2 pounds soup beef or chuck
10 cups water
3 cracked soup bones
1/2 pound lean fresh pork
1 bay leaf
8 peppercorns
2 sprigs parsley
1 garlic clove, halved
3 carrots, scraped and sliced
2 medium-sized onions, peeled and chopped
2 medium-sized leeks, white part only, washed and sliced
1/2 small head cabbage, coarsely chopped
3 medium-sized tomatoes, peeled and chopped
1-2 teaspoons sugar
1 cup sour cream at room temperature

Wash the beets and cook 7 of them, whole and unpeeled, in 1/4 cup vinegar and salted water to cover until tender, 30 to 40 minutes. Drain; peel and cut into julienne. Put the beef, bones and pork with 10 cups cold water in a large kettle. Bring to a boil. Skim well. Add the bay leaf, peppercorns, parsley, garlic, carrots, onions and leeks and cook slowly, covered, for 1½ hours, or until the meat is tender. Add the cooked beets, cabbage and tomatoes and continue to cook slowly for another 30 minutes, or until the ingredients are tender. Remove from the heat. Cut the meat into bite-sized pieces, discarding any bones and gristle, the bay leaf, peppercorns, parsley and garlic. Return the cut-up meat to the kettle. Season with salt. Peel and grate the remaining beet. Place in a saucepan with 1 cup of the hot soup stock, the remaining 1/4 cup of vinegar and sugar. Bring to a boil. Stir into the soup and warm up, if necessary. Ladle the soup into soup bowls and garnish with a spoonful of sour cream. Serves 8 to 10.

Note: Four peeled, cubed medium-sized potatoes may be added to the soup about 20 minutes before it is finished, if desired.

Korean Beef and Noodle Soup

Korean cookery is distinguished by its seasonings of sesame seeds or sesame oil, soy sauce, garlic, green onions, mono-sodium glutamate, and red and black pepper, all of which are used in soups as well as other dishes. In Korea, soup or *kook*, is eaten for all meals, including breakfast, and is a common snack. This is a good luncheon dish.

3 green onions with tops, sliced
1 garlic clove, crushed
2 tablespoons peanut or vegetable oil
1/2 pound lean beef, cut into tiny cubes
1 tablespoon sesame oil
3 tablespoons soy sauce
6 cups water or beef bouillon
1/2 teaspoon monosodium glutamate
pepper to taste
1½ cups broken Oriental or very fine egg noodles

Sauté the onions and garlic in the peanut or vegetable oil over low heat in a large kettle until the onions are tender. Push aside and add the meat, browning it on all sides. Add the sesame oil, soy sauce, bouillon, monosodium glutamate and pepper. Bring to a boil. Lower the heat and cook slowly, covered, about 40 minutes, or until the meat is tender. While the soup is cooking, boil the noodles in salted water until just tender; drain. Add to the soup and leave on the stove long enough to heat through. Serves 6 to 8.

Crisp Crackers
Sliced Pineapple with Coconut
Butter Cookies

Turkey Vegetable Soup with Macaroni

Practicality characterizes this soup, for it is nutritious, inexpensive, easy to prepare, and provides a solution for what to do with a leftover turkey carcass.

1 roast turkey carcass
8 cups water
1 medium-sized onion, peeled and chopped
1 cup diced celery
1/2 cup chopped celery leaves
1 bay leaf
2 parsley sprigs
salt, pepper to taste
2 cups elbow macaroni
2 cups chopped cooked turkey
1 can (1 pound) tomatoes, undrained
1 can (12 ounces) whole kernel corn
1/2 teaspoon dried basil
3 cups tomato juice
1 large green pepper, cleaned and chopped

Remove any stuffing from the turkey carcass and break up the carcass so it will fit into a large kettle. Add the water, onion, celery, celery leaves, bay leaf, parsley sprigs, salt and pepper. Bring to a boil. Lower the heat and cook slowly, covered, for 2 hours. Remove from the heat and let cool long enough so that the carcass can be easily removed. Cut any meat from the bones. Discard the bones and return the meat, chopped, to the soup kettle. Remove and discard the bay leaf and parsley sprigs. Cook the macaroni in salted boiling water until just tender. Drain and add to the soup. Add the tomatoes, corn and basil. Mix well. Pour in the tomato juice. Cook slowly over low heat for 15 minutes. Add the pepper 5 minutes before the cooking is finished. Serves 8.

MENU

Turkey Vegetable Soup with Macaroni
Warm Corn Muffins
Fresh Berries and Cream

Alsatian Frankfurter-Sauerkraut Soup

Some favorite foods of the picturesque French province of Alsace are combined to make a hearty soup—a good winter dinner dish.

1 medium-sized onion, peeled and chopped
3 tablespoons minced celery
3 tablespoons vegetable oil
1 can (16 ounces) sauerkraut, well drained
2 cups tomato juice
6 cups beef bouillon
or 6 beef bouillon cubes and 6 cups water
1/2 teaspoon dried thyme
1 large bay leaf
salt, pepper to taste
1 cup elbow macaroni
4 frankfurters, cut in 1/2-inch slices

Sauté the onion and celery in the oil in a kettle until tender. Add the sauerkraut and sauté, mixing with a fork, for 5 minutes. Add the tomato juice, bouillon, thyme, bay leaf, salt and pepper, and bring to a boil. Lower the heat and cook slowly, covered, for 30 minutes. Add the macaroni and frankfurters; raise the heat. Cook, uncovered, until the macaroni is tender, about 10 minutes. Remove and discard the bay leaf. Serves 8 to 10.

MENU

Alsatian Frankfurter-Sauerkraut Soup
Dark Rye Bread
Peach Shortcake

Tuna-Kale Supper Soup

Tuna and kale, a variety of cabbage, are both inexpensive and nourishing. In addition, the dark bluish-green leaves of kale have a high vitamin content. This is a good family supper dish.

1 package (10 ounces) frozen kale
1/2 cup chopped onion
2 tablespoons vegetable oil or margarine
1 can (10½ ounces) condensed cream of celery soup
4 cups hot milk
1 can (about 7 ounces) tuna, drained and flaked
2 cups cooked rice
2 tablespoons chopped fresh parsley
dash cayenne

Cook the kale according to the package directions. Drain and chop. Sauté the onion in the oil in a kettle until tender. Add the kale and other ingredients and heat gently. Serves 6.

MENU

Tuna-Kale Supper Soup
Warm Corn Muffins
Berry Cobbler

Viennese Beef-Vegetable Soup

Many fine soups have been created in the kitchens of Vienna. This staple hearty dish remains a favorite for all occasions.

1 large onion, peeled and chopped
1 large carrot, scraped and diced
1 large stalk celery, cleaned and chopped
2 large fresh or canned tomatoes, peeled and chopped
3 tablespoons vegetable oil or butter
2 pounds soup beef meat and bones

8 cups water
1/4 teaspoon dried basil or thyme
3 sprigs parsley
salt, pepper to taste
1/2 cup uncooked rice

In a large kettle combine the onion, carrot, celery, tomatoes and oil. Sauté the vegetables for 5 minutes. Push aside and add the soup meat and bones. Brown on all sides. Add the water, basil, parsley, salt and pepper. Bring to a boil. Lower the heat and cook slowly, covered, for 1 hour. Add the rice and continue to cook for another 30 minutes, or until the ingredients are cooked. Take out the meat and bones. Cut the meat into small pieces, removing and discarding any fat or gristle. Return to the soup. Serves 8.

MENU

Viennese Beef-Vegetable Soup
Poppy-Seed Rolls
Chocolate Layer Cake

Mushroom-Seafood Soup

An elegant soup for a weekend luncheon or late evening supper.

2 ounces salt pork, diced, or 2 slices bacon, chopped
1/2 cup sliced onions
2 cups diced raw potatoes
1/2 cup water
salt, pepper to taste
1/2 pound white fish fillets, cut-up
1 cup canned salmon, cleaned and flaked
3 cups light cream or milk
1 can (4 ounces) mushroom stems and pieces, drained
2 tablespoons chopped fresh parsley

Put the pork or bacon in a heavy kettle and fry until the fat is released. Mix in the onions and sauté until tender. Add the potatoes, water, salt and pepper. Cook, covered, over medium heat for 5 minutes. Add the fish pieces and continue cooking until the fish and potatoes are tender, about 8 minutes. Add the salmon, cream and mushrooms, and leave on the stove long enough to heat through. Serve garnished with the parsley. Serves 6.

MENU

Mushroom-Seafood Soup
Warm White Rolls
Lemon Meringue Pie

Barley-Vegetable Potage

Vegetarians or devotees of meatless dishes will like this nourishing, colorful thick soup.

2 medium-sized onions, peeled and diced
2 carrots, scraped and diced
2 stalks celery, cleaned and chopped
3 tablespoons butter or margarine
1 can (1 pound, 12 ounces) tomatoes, undrained
8 cups water
1 teaspoon dried basil
1/2 teaspoon dried thyme
salt, pepper to taste
1 cup pearl barley
2 cups cut frozen green beans or peas
1 tablespoon chopped fresh dill

In a large kettle sauté the onions, carrots and celery in the butter for 5 minutes. Add the tomatoes, water, basil, thyme, salt and pepper and bring to a boil. Stir in the barley and lower the heat. Cook slowly, covered, about 1½ hours, or until the barley is tender. Stir in the beans or peas during the last 10 minutes of cooking. Add the dill. Serves 10 to 12.

MENU

Barley-Vegetable Potage
Buttered English Muffins
Apple Cobbler

Bean-Macaroni Soup

This hearty thick soup, made with favorite southwestern foods, can be served as party fare or for a family meal.

2 cups (1 pound) dried pinto or kidney beans
8 cups water
2 teaspoons salt
1 large onion, peeled and chopped
2 tablespoons vegetable oil
1-2 tablespoons chili powder
1/2 teaspoon dried oregano
1 cup tomato sauce
pepper to taste
5 cups tomato juice
1½ cups frozen corn niblets
1½ cups elbow macaroni
1/2 cup minced green pepper

Put the beans and water in a large kettle and bring to a boil. Boil for 2 minutes. Remove from the heat. Let stand, covered, for 1 hour. Return to the heat and add the salt. Mix well and bring to a boil. Lower the heat and cook slowly, covered, for 1 hour. While the beans are cooking, sauté the onion in the oil in a small skillet until tender. Stir in the chili powder and oregano; cook 1 minute. Add the tomato sauce. Season with salt and pepper. Cook for 1 minute. When the beans have cooked for 1 hour, stir the onion-tomato mixture into the pot. Continue cooking for another 30 minutes. Add the tomato juice, corn and macaroni and cook about 15 minutes longer, or until the vegetables and macaroni are tender. Serve in a tureen or large bowl with the green pepper sprinkled over the cop. Serves 12.

MENU

Bean-Macaroni Soup
Warm Garlic Bread
Honey Spice Cake

Scandinavian Fisksoppa

Scandinavians enjoy many kinds of substantial fish soups and this is one of the best of them.

2 leeks, white parts only, cleaned and sliced
1/2 cup sliced onions
2 stalks celery, cleaned and sliced
3 medium-sized potatoes, cleaned and diced
1/3 cup butter or margarine
6 cups water
2 whole cloves
1/2 teaspoon ground nutmeg
salt, pepper to taste
1 pound white fish fillets (halibut, cod, haddock),
cut into bite-size pieces
1 can or jar (about 4 ounces) sliced mushrooms, drained
2 teaspoons chopped fresh dill or parsley

Sauté the leeks, onions, celery and potatoes in the butter for 5 minutes. Add the water, cloves, nutmeg, salt and pepper and cook 10 minutes. Add the fish fillets and cook until the fish and potatoes are just tender, about 12 minutes. Add the mushrooms 5 minutes before the cooking is finished. Serve garnished with the dill. Remove and discard the cloves. Serves 6 to 8.

MENU

Scandinavian Fisksoppa
Rye Bread
Rum Cream

Siamese Pork-Vegetable Pot

This Oriental creation is good fare for luncheon or dinner during any season.

2 pounds lean pork, cut in small cubes
3 tablespoons (about) peanut or vegetable oil
6 large green onions, chopped
2 garlic cloves, crushed
1/2 teaspoon ground coriander
dash cayenne
1-2 tablespoons soy sauce
pepper to taste
8 cups water
2 cups drained bamboo sprouts
2 cups sliced mushrooms
1/4 cup sliced water chestnuts
2 tablespoons chopped fresh parsley

Dry the pork cubes and brown in the oil in a large kettle. Push aside and add the onions, garlic and more oil, if needed. Sauté until tender. Add the coriander, cayenne, soy sauce and pepper. Pour in the water and bring to a boil. Lower the heat and cook slowly, covered, about 1½ hours, or until the pork is tender. Mix in the remaining ingredients 10 minutes before the cooking is finished. Serves 8.

MENU

Siamese Pork-Vegetable Pot
Crisp Crackers
Coconut Sprinkled Orange Sherbet

Sausage-Pasta Sopa

An easy-to-prepare Mexican-inspired soup that is even better if prepared beforehand and reheated.

1 large onion, peeled and chopped
1 tablespoon minced green chilies or green pepper
2 tablespoons vegetable oil
1½ cups canned tomatoes, chopped
pinch of sugar
salt, pepper to taste
6 cups tomato juice
2 *chorizo* sausages, skinned and cut into 1/2-inch slices,
or 1 cup smoked ham slivers
1 cup cooked green vegetables (peas, green beans)
2 cups cooked vermicelli

Sauté the onion and chilies in the oil in a kettle until tender. Stir in the tomatoes, sugar, salt and pepper. Cook for 5 minutes. Add the tomato juice and sausages. Bring to a boil. Lower the heat and cook slowly, covered, for 15 minutes. Add the vegetables and vermicelli, and leave on the stove long enough to heat through. Serves 6.

MENU

Sausage-Pasta Sopa
Warm Corn Bread
Caramel Custard

Winter Pea-Sausage Soup

This inexpensive and nourishing soup is good for lunch or supper.

2 cups (1 pound) green split peas
2 medium-sized onions, peeled and diced
2 carrots, scraped and diced
2 stalks celery, cleaned and sliced thinly
3 tablespoons butter or margarine
10 cups water
salt, pepper to taste
1/2 teaspoon dried thyme

1/2 teaspoon dried oregano
dash cayenne
1 pound sausage links, fried and sliced thickly
2 tablespoons minced fresh parsley

Rinse the peas. Sauté the onions, carrots and celery in the butter in a large kettle for 5 minutes. Add the water and bring to a boil. Season with salt and pepper. Add the thyme, oregano and cayenne and cook slowly, covered, for about 1 hour, or until the peas are tender. Mix in the sausage and parsley. Excellent if reheated the next day. Serves 8.

MENU

Winter Pea-Sausage Soup
Crusty Dark Bread
Warm Cherry Strudel

Tuna and Shell Chowder

This seafood chowder usually makes a hit when served on a cold, wintry night.

2 cups small pasta shells
3 tablespoons butter or margarine
2 cans (about 7 ounces each) tuna
2 tablespoons minced green onions with tops
2 tablespoons tomato paste
1/8 teaspoon cayenne
salt, pepper to taste
6 cups milk
1/3 cup chopped fresh parsley

Cook and drain the shells. Melt the butter in a large saucepan and add the oil from the tuna. Stir in the green onions and sauté until tender. Add the tomato paste, cayenne, salt and pepper. Cook, stirring, for 1 minute. Add the tuna and then the milk. Cook over a low flame to heat. Stir in the cooked shells and parsley, and leave on the stove long enough to heat through. Serves 6 to 8.

MENU

Tuna and Shell Chowder
Warm Biscuits
Coffee Parfait

Indian Lamb-Rice Soup

Inexpensive breast of lamb is combined with rice and peas to make a good dinner soup.

2 pounds breast of lamb, cut up
2 tablespoons peanut or vegetable oil
8 cups water
salt, pepper to taste
1 large onion, peeled and chopped
2 tablespoons butter or margarine
2-3 tablespoons curry powder
2/3 cup uncooked rice
1 can (6 ounces) tomato paste
2 cups frozen green peas

Wipe the lamb dry and brown in the oil in a heavy kettle. Pour off the fat. Add the water, salt and pepper and bring to a boil. Lower the heat and simmer, covered, for about 1 hour, or until the lamb is cooked. Remove from the stove and take out the lamb. Remove the meat from the bones and return it to the kettle, discarding fat and bones. In a small skillet sauté the onion in the butter until tender. Mix in the curry powder; cook 1 minute. Add this mixture, the tomato paste and rice to the soup and continue cooking about 30 minutes longer, or until the rice is cooked. Mix in the peas about 10 minutes before the cooking is finished. Serves 6 to 8.

MENU

Indian Lamb-Rice Soup
Warm Whole-Wheat Rolls
Orange Cream Pie

Corn-Tomato Chowder

This is a good Sunday supper dish from New England.

2 tablespoons diced salt pork, bacon, or vegetable oil
1 small onion, peeled and minced
1 tablespoon diced green pepper
2 cups (1 pound can) tomatoes
1/2 teaspoon crumbled dried basil or thyme
salt, pepper to taste
1 package (10 ounces) frozen cut corn
3 cups milk
1 teaspoon sugar
3 tablespoons chopped fresh parsley

Combine the pork, onion and green pepper in a kettle and sauté 2 to 3 minutes. Add the tomatoes, basil, salt and pepper. Cook slowly for 10 minutes. Mix in the corn, milk and sugar and cook slowly without boiling about 10 minutes longer, until the corn is tender. Serve garnished with the parsley. Serves 4.

MENU

Corn-Tomato Chowder
Warm Parkerhouse Rolls
Deep-Dish Apple Pie

Russian Vegetable Soup

In Russia many popular soups are made with cabbage. This one is also rich in other vegetables and is a good winter dish.

1 large onion, peeled and sliced
1 leek, white part only, cleaned and sliced
2 carrots, scraped and cut 1/4 inch thick
1 large stalk celery, cleaned and chopped
1/2 turnip, peeled and cubed
3 tablespoons bacon fat or shortening
8 cups beef bouillon
1 head green cabbage, about 1½ pounds,
cored, cleaned and shredded
1 can (6 ounces) tomato paste
3 tablespoons chopped fresh dill or parsley

Sauté the onion, leek, carrots, celery and turnip in bacon fat for 5 minutes. Add the bouillon and bring to a boil. Stir in the cabbage and tomato paste. Reduce the heat. Cook slowly, covered, for about 1 hour, until the vegetables are cooked. Sprinkle with dill or parsley. Serves 6 to 8.

MENU

Russian Vegetable Soup
Buttered Black Bread
Cherry Tarts

Portuguese Green Soup

Native to Portugal's northwest region of Minho, this green soup is made with a deep green kale which is unlike that grown elsewhere. Kale or spinach found in American stores can be used as a substitute.

1 pound fresh kale
4 medium-sized potatoes, pared
8 cups water
1/4 cup olive or vegetable oil
salt, pepper to taste
1/2 pound smoked garlic sausage, cooked and sliced into
1/4-inch rounds

Wash the kale and cut off any stems. Slice into thin shreds. Put the potatoes, water, oil, salt and pepper in a saucepan and bring to a boil. Lower the heat and cook slowly, covered, for about 25 minutes, or until the potatoes are tender. Remove from the stove, and put the mixture through a sieve or purée it. Return to the saucepan; add the strips of kale. Continue to cook about 12 minutes longer, or until the kale is tender. Add the sausage rounds, and leave on the stove long enough to heat through. Serves 6.

MENU

Portuguese Green Soup
Warm Garlic Bread
Baked Bananas in Orange Juice

Turkish Cauliflower-Shrimp Soup

A soup that was created in the sultan's palace is still unusual fare worthy of a special occasion.

1 medium head cauliflower
salt
2 tablespoons lemon juice
3 tablespoons butter or margarine
1/3 cup minced green onions with tops
2 tablespoons flour
4 cups hot chicken broth
2 cups light cream or milk
freshly ground pepper and grated nutmeg to taste

3 tablespoons grated mild cheese
2 cups cooked shelled shrimp

Wash the cauliflower. Cut off the stem and tough outer leaves. Cook, covered, in a little boiling salted water with the lemon juice, until tender, about 15 minutes. Drain; cut into small pieces. Melt the butter in a kettle. Add the onions and sauté until tender. Stir in the flour and cook 1 minute. Gradually add the chicken broth, stirring constantly, and then add the cream. Season with salt, pepper and nutmeg. Mix in the cheese and shrimp and cook slowly, stirring, until the sauce thickens and the cheese melts. Add the cauliflower pieces a few minutes before removing from the heat. Serves 6 to 8.

MENU

Turkish Cauliflower-Shrimp Soup
Crusty Dark Bread
Cheesecake

Maine Fish Chowder

Since colonial days, this simple but nourishing soup has been a staple supper dish in Maine.

1/4 pound salt pork, diced
3 medium-sized onions, peeled and sliced
4 cups diced raw potatoes
salt to taste
hot water
2 pounds cod or haddock fillets, cut into 1-inch pieces
2 cups milk, scalded
1 tablespoon butter or margarine
pepper to taste
6 large soda crackers, split in half

Fry the salt pork in a kettle. Add the onions and cook until tender. Add the potatoes, salt and hot water to cover. Cook, covered, for 10 minutes. Add the fish and continue to cook for about 8 minutes, or until the fish flakes easily and the potatoes are tender. Add the milk and leave on the stove long enough to heat through. Mix in the butter and pepper. Serve in soup bowls over halved crackers. Serves 6.

MENU

Maine Fish Chowder
Warm Johnnycake or Corn Muffins
Blueberry Pie

Herbed Broccoli Bisque

This is an excellent dish for a light meal.

2 packages (10 ounces each) frozen chopped broccoli
1 medium-sized onion, peeled and minced
1/4 cup butter or margarine
2 tablespoons flour
4 cups chicken broth
1 teaspoon dried basil or oregano
1/2 cup chopped fresh parsley
salt, pepper to taste
1 cup small pasta (alphabets, ditalini,
cut-up spaghetti)
2 cups light cream or milk

Cook the broccoli in a little water according to package directions and set aside. Sauté the onion in the butter in a large saucepan until tender. Mix in the flour and cook 1 minute. Add the broth, basil, parsley, salt and pepper and bring to a boil. Lower the heat and cook slowly, covered, for 10 minutes. Meanwhile, cook the pasta until just tender and drain. Add the pasta, broccoli and cream or milk to the chicken broth mixture. Heat gently for 5 minutes. Serves 8.

MENU

Herbed Broccoli Bisque
Warm Garlic Bread
Chocolate Cream Pie

Vietnamese Beef-Noodle Soup

A national dish of Vietnam made with beef, noodles and seasonings is called *pho* or *po* and is eaten as a snack or quick meal. This is an easy-to-prepare version of the original recipe.

2 pounds soup bones
1 pound stew beef, cut into large cubes
1 large onion
1 large garlic clove, crushed
1 tablespoon chopped fresh ginger
1/2 teaspoon crushed aniseed
1/2 teaspoon monosodium glutamate
1½ cups water
salt, pepper to taste
1/4 pound fine egg noodles
6 green onions, with tops, sliced
1 teaspoon anchovy paste
1 teaspoon vinegar
chili powder to taste

Put the soup bones and beef in a large kettle. Cut the onion in half and slice thinly. Add, with the garlic, ginger, aniseed, monosodium glutamate, water, salt and pepper, to the meat. Bring to a boil. Lower the heat and cook slowly, covered, for 1½ hours. Add more water during cooking, if needed. Remove from the heat. Take out and discard the bones. Take out the meat and cut into small pieces. Return to the kettle. Cook the noodles in boiling water until just tender. Drain and add with the green onions to the broth and meat. Combine the anchovy paste, vinegar and chili powder and stir into the meat mixture. Leave on the stove long enough to heat through. Serves 6.

MENU

Vietnamese Beef-Noodle Soup
Sesame Crackers
Pineapple-Orange Compote

Creole Tomato-Rice Soup

Colorful Creole foods are used to make this flavorful vegetable soup enhanced with rice.

1 medium-sized onion, peeled and chopped
1/2 cup diced green pepper
1/2 cup diced celery
3 tablespoons butter or margarine
3 tablespoons all-purpose flour
3 cups chicken broth
1 can (1 pound) tomatoes
1 small bay leaf
1/2 teaspoon dried thyme
salt, pepper to taste
1/3 cup uncooked long grain rice
1 cup frozen cut-up okra
dash hot pepper sauce

Sauté the onion, pepper and celery in the butter in a large saucepan or kettle for 5 minutes. Stir in the flour and cook 1 minute. Gradually add the chicken broth, stirring constantly. Mix in the tomatoes and break up with a fork or spoon. Add the bay leaf, thyme, salt, pepper and rice and cook slowly, covered, for 30 minutes. Stir in the okra and hot pepper sauce and cook about 5 minutes longer, or until the ingredients are tender. Serves 6.

MENU

Creole Tomato-Rice Soup
Corn Sticks
Coffee Chiffon Pie

Dinner Beef-Macaroni Soup

The family will welcome this soup for a weekday dinner.

1 medium-sized onion, peeled and chopped
2 tablespoons vegetable oil
1-2 tablespoons chili powder
1 pound lean ground beef
6 tablespoons tomato paste
1 teaspoon paprika
salt, pepper to taste
8 cups beef bouillon
2 cans (15 ounces each) chili beans or
kidney beans, drained
2 cups small macaroni, cooked and drained
1/2 cup chopped fresh parsley

Sauté the onion in the oil in a kettle until tender. Stir in the chili powder and cook 1 minute. Add the ground beef and cook, mincing with a fork, until the redness disappears. Stir in the tomato paste, paprika, salt and pepper. Add the bouillon and bring to a boil. Lower the heat and cook slowly, covered, for 15 minutes. Add the beans and cooked macaroni and heat gently for 5 minutes. Serve garnished with the parsley. Serves 8.

MENU

Dinner Beef-Macaroni Soup
Warm Corn Bread
Apricot Upside-Down Cake

Finnish Summer Vegetable Soup

This soup, called *kesakeitto* in Finland, is made with garden-fresh vegetables when they are at their peak. It also can be made with a combination of fresh and frozen ones.

2 cups thinly sliced onions
1 cup thinly sliced carrots
2 cups diced potatoes
2 cups cut-up cauliflower
2 cups cut-up green beans
1 cup shelled fresh or frozen green peas
5 cups boiling water
1 tablespoon sugar
salt, pepper to taste
6 tablespoons flour
6 cups hot milk
2 tablespoons butter or margarine
1/3 cup chopped fresh parsley

Put the vegetables and boiling water in a large kettle. Add the sugar, salt and pepper and bring to a boil. Lower the heat and cook slowly, covered, until the vegetables are just tender, about 20 minutes. Meanwhile, combine the flour and milk and mix until smooth. Pour into the kettle and mix well. Cook slowly, stirring, for a few minutes. Remove from the heat, and add the butter and parsley. Serves 8.

MENU

Finnish Summer Vegetable Soup
Buttered French Bread
Jam-Filled Pancakes

The following six soups can be easily made and are superb for family or company meals. Canned soups and other familiar foods kept regularly on the kitchen shelves are included among the ingredients.

Bean-Ham Pot

1/4 cup chopped onions
1/4 cup chopped green pepper
2 tablespoons butter or margarine

2 cups diced cooked ham
1 can (11½ ounces) condensed ˙ean with bacon soup
1 can (10¾ ounces) condensed tomato soup
1 soup can water
3 soup cans milk
1 teaspoon Worcestershire sauce
croutons

Sauté the onions and green peppers in the butter in a large saucepan until tender. Add the ham and sauté 1 minute. Mix in the soups, water, milk and Worcestershire sauce Heat gently. Serve with croutons. Serves 4 to 6.

MENU

Bean-Ham Pot
Nut Muffins
Banana Cream Pie

Continental Chicken-Mushroom Pot

2 cans (10½ ounces each) condensed
cream of chicken soup
2 cans (10½ ounces each) condensed
cream of mushroom soup
3 soup cans milk
1 soup can chicken broth or water
1/4 teaspoon dried basil
4 cups diced cooked chicken
2 cups frozen green peas
2 cups cooked egg noodles
salt, pepper to taste
2 tablespoons chopped fresh parsley

In a large saucepan combine the soups, milk, chicken broth and basil and heat gently. Mix in the chicken, peas, noodles, salt and pepper and cook slowly, covered, for another 5 minutes or until the peas are tender. Serve garnished with the parsley. Serves 8.

MENU

Continental Chicken-Mushroom Pot
Hot Whole-Wheat Rolls
French Pastry

Southern Company Seafood Chowder

1/4 cup chopped onion
1/4 cup chopped celery
1/2 cup chopped green pepper
2 tablespoons butter or margarine
1 can (10½ ounces) condensed cream of potato soup
2 soup cans milk
1 can (10 ounces) frozen condensed cream of shrimp soup
2 cups flaked tuna fish
1/2 teaspoon dried basil or thyme
salt, pepper to taste
croutons

In a saucepan sauté the onion, celery and green pepper in the butter until tender. Add the remaining ingredients, except the croutons, and heat gently until the shrimp soup is thawed and the ingredients are hot. Do not boil. Serve garnished with croutons. Serves 4.

MENU

Southern Company Seafood Chowder
Buttered Toasted English Muffins
Peach Pie

Hearty Frankfurter-Tomato Tureen

4 frankfurters, thinly sliced
1 tablespoon butter or margarine
1 can (1 pound) tomatoes, undrained

1 can (10¾ ounces) condensed tomato soup
1 soup can milk
1/8 teaspoon dried rosemary or basil
salt, pepper to taste
2 cups cooked elbow macaroni

In a saucepan brown the frankfurter slices in butter. Add the tomatoes and cook, breaking with a spoon, for 1 or 2 minutes. Add the soup, milk, rosemary, salt and pepper and heat gently, stirring, for 5 minutes. Mix in the macaroni and leave on the stove long enough to heat through. Serves 4.

MENU

Hearty Frankfurter-Tomato Tureen
Hot Buttered French Bread
Pineapple Upside-Down Cake

Mexican Chili-Beef Soup

1 large onion, peeled and chopped
1 garlic clove, crushed (optional)
2 tablespoons vegetable oil
1-2 tablespoons chili powder
1 pound lean ground beef
1/4 teaspoon dried oregano
salt, pepper to taste
1 can (1 pound, 12 ounces) tomatoes, undrained
3 cups beef bouillon or water
1 can (1 pound) kidney beans, drained
1 medium-sized green pepper, cleaned and minced

In a large saucepan sauté the onion and garlic in the oil until tender. Add the chili powder and cook 1 minute. Mix in the beef and cook, stirring with a fork, until the redness disappears. Add the oregano, salt and pepper. Add the tomatoes and bouillon, and cook slowly, uncovered, for 20 minutes. Break up the tomatoes with the back of a spoon.

Mix in the beans and green pepper and leave on the stove until the beans are heated. Serves 4 to 6.

MENU

Mexican Chili-Beef Soup
Warm Corn Muffins
Orange Sherbet With Chocolate Sauce

Lamb-Hominy Soup with Corn

1/3 cup chopped onion
2 tablespoons vegetable oil
1-2 tablespoons curry powder
2 cups diced cooked lamb
1 can (1 pound) tomatoes, undrained
1 can (11¼ ounces) condensed green pea soup
1 soup can milk
1 can (1 pound) hominy
2 cups frozen or canned corn niblets
2 tablespoons chopped fresh parsley

In a large saucepan sauté the onion in the oil. Mix in the curry powder and cook 1 minute. Add the lamb and tomatoes, and cook, breaking with a spoon, for 1 minute. Add the pea soup and milk and heat gently, stirring often. Add the hominy and corn, and leave on the stove long enough for the corn to be tender. Serve garnished with the parsley. Serves 6.

MENU

Lamb-Hominy Soup with Corn
Whole-Wheat Bread
Vanilla Ice Cream with Pineapple Topping

This is a group of eight light soups that can be served by themselves or with open-faced sandwiches for luncheons or light suppers.

Potage Crème de Tomates

3 cups chopped ripe tomatoes
2 tablespoons minced onion
1 small bay leaf
1/4 teaspoon celery seed
3 whole cloves
salt, pepper to taste
2 tablespoons butter or margarine
2 tablespoons all-purpose flour
2 cups light cream or milk
1/4 cup dry sherry (optional)

In a large saucepan combine the tomatoes, onion, bay leaf, celery seed, cloves, salt and pepper. Cook slowly, covered, for 15 minutes. Press through a sieve or strainer. In a large saucepan melt the butter and stir in the flour to form a *roux*. Gradually add the cream or milk, and cook slowly, stirring almost constantly, until smooth and thickened. Stir in the tomato mixture and continue to cook slowly another 5 minutes. Remove from the heat and stir in the sherry. Serves 4.

MENU

Potage Crème de Tomates
Sliced Ham and Lettuce on Rye Bread
Brownies with Ice Cream

Near Eastern Cucumber-Yogurt Soup

4 cups plain yogurt
2 garlic cloves, crushed
2 medium-sized cucumbers, peeled, seeded and chopped

1/2 cup chopped walnuts (optional)
1 tablespoon wine vinegar
salt, pepper to taste
2 tablespoons olive or vegetable oil
1 tablespoon chopped fresh mint or parsley

In a large bowl beat the yogurt smooth. Add the garlic, cucumbers, walnuts, vinegar, salt and pepper and mix well. Chill. To serve, spoon into small bowls or cups and garnish with a little oil and mint or parsley. Serves 4.

MENU

Near Eastern Cucumber-Yogurt Soup
Cold Roast Lamb or Beef and Lettuce on White Bread
Warm Nut Cake with Lemon Sauce

Gazpacho

Although there are many recipes for this popular Spanish summer soup, this is an Andalusian version that is served in Seville.

1-2 garlic cloves
salt to taste
1 cup soft bread cubes, crusts removed
1/4 cup wine vinegar
4 medium-sized ripe tomatoes, peeled and chopped
1 medium-sized cucumber, peeled, seeded and chopped
1 large pepper, cleaned and diced
1/4 cup olive or vegetable oil
2 cups cold water
2 cups tomato juice
pepper
garnishes: chopped green onions, toasted bread cubes

Pound the garlic and salt in a mortar with a pestle or in a bowl with a wooden spoon. Add the bread cubes and vinegar and work into a paste. Add 3 of the tomatoes and 1/2 the cucumber and mash as fine as possible or whirl in a blender. Mix with the remaining chopped tomato, cucumber and diced pepper. Chill. Before serving stir in the oil, water and tomato juice. Add more vinegar, if desired. Season with salt and pepper. Serve with garnishes, if desired. Serves 6.

MENU

Gazpacho
Grilled Swiss Cheese on White Bread
Orange Custard

Cream of Mushroom Potage

1 pound fresh mushrooms
5 tablespoons butter or margarine
1 tablespoon fresh lemon juice
salt, pepper to taste
2 tablespoons minced shallots or green onions
3 tablespoons minced onions
2 tablespoons flour
6 cups chicken broth
1 bay leaf
2 parsley sprigs
dash cayenne
1 cup light cream or milk

Clean the mushrooms by rinsing quickly or wiping with a damp paper towel to remove any dirt. Pull the stems from the caps and cut off any tough stem ends. Chop the stems finely. Slice the caps. In a large saucepan melt 2 tablespoons of butter. Add the sliced caps and lemon juice and sauté 3 minutes. Season with salt and pepper and remove to a plate.

Melt the remaining 3 tablespoons of butter in a saucepan. Add the shallots and onions and sauté until tender. Mix in the chopped mushroom stems and sauté 2 minutes. Stir in the flour and cook over low heat, stirring constantly, 1 or 2 minutes. Gradually add the chicken broth, stirring as adding. Mix in the bay leaf, parsley, cayenne, salt and pepper. Cook over low heat, stirring often, for 15 minutes. Strain, pressing the mushrooms with a spoon to release all the juices. Return the strained liquid to the saucepan. Add the sautéed sliced mushrooms and drippings and the cream or milk. Leave on the stove long enough to heat through. Serves 6.

MENU

Cream of Mushroom Potage
Sliced Egg and Bacon on Whole-Wheat Bread
Chocolate Eclairs

Vichyssoise

4 leeks, white parts only, cleaned and sliced
1 medium-sized onion, peeled and sliced thinly
1/4 cup butter or margarine
5 medium-sized potatoes, peeled and sliced
4 cups chicken broth or water
salt to taste
4 cups light cream or milk
white pepper to taste
1 cup heavy cream
chopped chives

Sauté the leeks and onion in the butter in a saucepan until tender. Add the potatoes, chicken broth or water, and salt. Bring to a boil. Lower the heat and cook gently, covered, about 30 minutes, or until tender. Purée or whirl in a blender. Return to the stove and gradually add the cream or milk. Bring just to a boil. Remove at once from the heat. Cool. Put through a sieve. Season with salt and pepper. Add the heavy cream and chill thoroughly. Serve garnished with chopped chives. Serves 8.

MENU

Vichyssoise
Sliced Turkey and Tomato on Pumpernickel
Orange Chiffon Cake

Consommé Julienne

1/2 cup sliced green onions
1 tablespoon butter or margarine
2 tablespoons tomato paste
4 cups beef consommé
salt, pepper to taste
1 cup cooked vegetables (carrots, string beans, celery,
green peppers), cut into julienne
2 cups cooked and drained small pasta
(alphabets, pastina)

In a large saucepan sauté the onions in the butter until tender. Stir in the tomato paste. Add the consommé, salt and pepper, and bring to a boil. Lower the heat and cook slowly, covered, for 10 minutes. Mix in the vegetables and pasta and leave on the stove long enough to heat through. Serves 4.

MENU

Consommé Julienne
Sliced Chicken and Lettuce on Whole-Wheat Bread
Coconut Cream Pie

Carrot Potage

1 small onion, peeled and diced
1 small potato, peeled and diced
2 cups chopped carrots

2½ cups consommé or water
1/2 teaspoon sugar
1/2 teaspoon dried thyme or marjoram
salt, pepper to taste
2 tablespoons butter or margarine
2 tablespoons flour
3 cups milk
1 cup light cream
1 tablespoon minced fresh mint, dill or parsley

In a saucepan cook the onion, potato, carrots, consommé, sugar, thyme, salt and pepper until the carrots are tender, about 30 minutes. Put through a sieve or whirl in a blender until smooth. Melt the butter in a saucepan. Mix in the flour to form a *roux*. Gradually add the milk, stirring constantly, and cook until thick and smooth. Stir in the carrot purée and cook slowly until heated. Add the cream and leave on the stove long enough to heat through. Serve garnished with the herbs. Serves 6.

MENU

Carrot Potage
Sliced Ham and Lettuce on White Bread
Fresh Berries
Nut Cookies

Cream of Asparagus Soup

1 package (10 ounces) frozen asparagus spears
3 tablespoons minced onion
2 cups chicken bouillon
2 tablespoons butter or margarine
2 tablespoons flour
2 cups milk
1 cup light or heavy cream
salt, pepper to taste
dash nutmeg

Cook the asparagus according to the package directions until tender. Drain, reserving 1/2 cup of the liquid. Cut the asparagus into small pieces, reserving the tips. Combine the asparagus, 1/2 cup of the liquid, onion and bouillon in a saucepan and cook over medium heat for 5 minutes. Purée in a blender. In another saucepan melt the butter. Mix in the flour and cook 1 minute. Slowly add the milk, stirring constantly, and cook until thick and smooth. Stir in the asparagus purée, cream, salt and pepper, and leave on the stove long enough to heat through. Add the nutmeg and serve garnished with the asparagus tips. Serves 4 to 6.

MENU

Cream of Asparagus Soup
Tuna or Salmon and Lettuce on White Bread
Fresh Fruit Tarts

South American Supper Soup

This colorful soup is made with a medley of favorite South American foods—beef, tomatoes, potatoes, corn, green beans and chickpeas.

1 pound stew meat, cut in small cubes
1 large onion, peeled and chopped
1-2 garlic cloves, crushed
3-4 tablespoons vegetable oil
2 large tomatoes, peeled and chopped
1 teaspoon crumbled dried oregano
salt, pepper to taste
8 cups beef consommé or water
3 medium-sized potatoes, peeled and cubed
2 cups frozen corn
2 cups frozen cut-up green beans
1 can (1 pound, 4 ounces) chickpeas, drained
2 tablespoons chopped fresh parsley

Dry the meat. In a large kettle sauté the onion and garlic in the oil until tender. Push aside and add the meat. Brown on all sides. Add the tomatoes, oregano, salt and pepper and cook briskly for 5 minutes. Pour in the consommé or water and bring to a boil. Lower the heat and cook slowly, covered, for 1 hour. Add the potatoes and continue cooking about 30 minutes longer, or until the ingredients are tender. Mix in the remaining ingredients during the last 10 minutes of cooking. Serves 8.

MENU

South American Supper Soup
Warm Corn Muffins
Coconut Cream Pie

Basque Vegetable Soup

This hearty soup is made with favorite foods of the Basque region in northern Spain.

1 cup dried navy beans, washed
salt
8 cups water
1 large onion, peeled and chopped
2 garlic cloves, crushed
2 tablespoons olive or vegetable oil
1 can (6 ounces) tomato paste
2 medium-sized bay leaves
1/2 teaspoon dried oregano
pepper to taste
3 medium-sized potatoes, peeled and cubed
3 small zucchini, stemmed and cubed
3 cups shredded green cabbage

Put the beans in lightly salted water in a large kettle and bring to a boil. Boil for 2 minutes. Remove from the heat and let stand for 1 hour. Bring again to a boil and simmer, covered, for 1 hour. Meanwhile, sauté the onion and garlic in the oil in a small skillet until tender. Add the onion, garlic and the remaining ingredients to the beans, and continue cooking about 40 minutes or until the ingredients are tender. Remove and discard the bay leaves. Serves 8 to 10.

MENU

Basque Vegetable Soup
Warm Garlic Bread
Cheese Plate

STEWS

Since people first began devising mixtures of their favorite foods to be cooked in pots, there has been a close affinity between soups and stews. In fact they have been so closely allied that it is still difficult to make a distinction between them. Spain's *olla podrida* is called a soup and a stew. Suffice it to say that both dishes are made of cut-up ingredients cooked in liquid, but a stew is generally simmered longer and slower, and has less liquid.

Over the years, stews have ranked high in our diet, but unfortunately their reputation has sometimes suffered. Too often many persons merely think of a stew as uninspired mundane fare to be eaten as a last choice. Nothing could be further from the truth. Stews are actually gastronomic delights of fascinating variety that can be proudly served on any occasion.

The earliest stews were made with bits of meat or game with legumes and perhaps vegetables and seasonings. They provided necessary sustenance. Trying to improve them, the Romans combined bizarre mixtures so heavily spiced that the taste of the foods was disguised. Yet they did create the early versions of fricassees and ragouts.

To the French we are indebted for the refinements of stewing foods. By the twelfth century French chefs had succeeded in converting basic dishes to more sophisticated fare and bequeathed to the world the glorious *blanquettes, daubes, navarins, matelotes*, fricassees and ragouts—all stews.

One could travel around the world just sampling national stews, important to every cuisine. Cooks in other lands created such well-known kinds as goulashes, or the ubiquitous stew known variously as *stifado, estofado* or *estouffade*, to name only a few.

As stews, particularly those from foreign lands, have become more and more popular on the American table so have the array of utensils for cooking them. Although any heavy pot of the right size is adequate, many persons delight in using fancier kinds of varying shapes and colors. Some of the most attractive are imported and have such esoteric-sounding names as *daubière* or *braisière*. Most are so appealing that the stew can be served as well as cooked in the pot.

It's great fun to entertain with stews—they generate an informal or casual mood, and the serving can be most flexible, either with informal or formal appointments. Often the hostess can create a particular atmosphere with the table decor to fit in with the theme of a foreign menu or a particular occasion. Stews are perfect for buffets, dinners or suppers, as well as noon-time meals. The following recipes with menu suggestions will be rewarding to cook and serve.

Blanquette de Veau

Of French origin, this well-known, lemon-flavored veal stew with small white onions and fresh mushrooms is superb fare. It takes some time and effort to prepare, and except for the final addition of egg yolks and cream, it can be made ahead and reheated just before the meal. It is excellent for a company dinner.

2½ pounds boneless veal shoulder, cut into 2-inch cubes
4 cups beef bouillon or water
1 carrot, scraped and chopped
1 medium-sized onion stuck with 2 whole cloves
1 leek, white part only, cleaned and sliced (optional)
bouquet garni **(1 bay leaf, 1/2 teaspoon dried thyme,**
2 parsley sprigs)
salt, pepper to taste
5 tablespoons butter
16 small white onions, peeled
1/2 cup water
18 fresh mushrooms
2 tablespoons fresh lemon juice
3 tablespoons flour
2 egg yolks
1/2 cup heavy cream
freshly grated nutmeg to taste

Put the veal and bouillon in a large kettle. Bring to a boil and skim. Add the carrot, onion with cloves, leek, *bouquet garni*, salt and pepper. Lower the heat and cook slowly, covered, for 1½ hours, skimming from time to time. While the veal is cooking, melt 1 tablespoon butter in a saucepan. Add the white onions and sauté 1 minute. Pour in the water and cook the onions, covered, until just tender, about 10 minutes. Drain and set aside. Clean the mushrooms and cut into halves lengthwise. Sauté in 2 tablespoons butter and 1 tablespoon lemon juice for 5 minutes. Remove from the heat and set aside. When the veal has finished cooking, remove from the stove. Take out the meat. Strain 2 cups of the liquid and set aside. (Discard any remaining liquid and the vegetables in which the veal was cooked.) Melt 2 table-spoons butter in a large saucepan. Add the flour and cook, stirring, one minute. Gradually add the strained meat liquid and cook, stirring, until the sauce is thickened and smooth. Combine the egg yolks and cream and beat lightly. Mix a small amount of the hot sauce with the egg yolks. Return the mixture to the sauce. Cook slowly, stirring often, until thickened. Season with salt, pepper and nutmeg. Add the reserved veal, onions, mushrooms and drippings and the remaining 1 table-spoon of lemon juice. Leave on the stove long enough to heat through. Serves 6.

MENU

Blanquette de Veau
Buttered Noodles
Mixed Green Salad
French Pastry

Hungarian Pork Tokany

In the superb repertoire of Hungarian stews, one of the best is called *tokany*. A paprika-flavored pork or beef dish for which the meat is cut into strips, a *tokany* also includes mush-rooms, vegetables and sour cream.

2 pounds lean boneless pork, cut into
3-by-1-inch strips
1/4 cup lard or shortening
salt, pepper to taste
1 tablespoon paprika
1 large onion, peeled and chopped
1 large carrot, scraped and sliced thinly
1 large green pepper, cleaned and sliced
2 medium-sized tomatoes, peeled and chopped
2 cups sliced fresh mushrooms
1 tablespoon flour
1 cup sour cream, at room temperature

Wipe the pork dry and brown it in the lard in a large sauce-pan. Season with salt and pepper. Add the paprika and onion and cook 1 minute. Cover and cook slowly for 30 minutes. Add the carrot, pepper and tomatoes and cook another 30 minutes or until tender. Stir in the mushrooms 10 minutes before the cooking is finished. Add the flour and sour cream and cook over low heat, stirring, until thickened and smooth, about 5 minutes. Serves 6.

MENU

Hungarian Pork Tokany
Buttered Noodles
Wilted Cucumber Salad
Warm Poppy-Seed Rolls
Fruit-Filled Pancakes

Turkish Gardeners' Stew

The Turks prepare a marvelous stew called *turlu*, which is made from lamb and a medley of vegetables. The choice of vegetables will vary as to what is in season and available, but the ones in this recipe are a typical selection. It is a good summer dinner dish.

4 medium-sized onions, peeled and sliced
1/2 cup butter or margarine
2 pounds boneless shoulder or leg of lamb, cut into
1-inch cubes
salt, pepper to taste
4 medium-sized zucchini, washed and sliced
2 medium-sized eggplant, stemmed and cubed
1 pound fresh green beans, stemmed and cut up
1/2 pound fresh okra, stemmed and cut up
4 large tomatoes, peeled and chopped

Sauté the onions in the butter in a large kettle until tender. Wipe the lamb dry and brown on all sides. Season with salt and pepper. Cover with about 1/2 cup water and cook slowly for about 1 hour. Add more water while cooking if necessary to prevent sticking. Add the prepared vegetables and continue to cook slowly, covered, about 30 minutes longer or until the ingredients are cooked. Serves 6.

MENU

Turkish Gardeners' Stew
Hot Boiled Rice
Crusty Dark Bread
Chilled Watermelon

Philippine Adobo

The Filipinos have a rich heritage of national stews which are served traditionally at festive meals. This highly seasoned chicken and pork *adobo* is better if prepared two or three days in advance and reheated.

1 frying chicken, about 2½ pounds, cut up
2 pounds boneless pork loin or shoulder, cut into
1-inch cubes
1 cup wine vinegar
1/2 cup soy sauce
2 bay leaves
2-3 garlic cloves
1 teaspoon peppercorns, slightly bruised
salt to taste
lard or oil for frying
1 cup coconut milk*

Put the chicken pieces, pork, vinegar, soy sauce, bay leaves, garlic, peppercorns and salt in a large kettle, cover and leave to marinate at room temperature for 1½ to 2 hours. Put the mixture on the stove and bring to a boil. Lower the heat, cover and cook very slowly for about 45 minutes or until the meat is tender. Remove the pork and chicken and drain. Strain the liquid and reserve. Fry the pork cubes and chicken in the lard or oil to brown on all sides. Return the liquid to the kettle. Add the coconut milk and cook slowly about 10 minutes longer, or until the mixture thickens. Serves 8.
*See recipe on page 113.

MENU

Philippine Adobo
Hot Cooked Rice
Warm Corn Sticks
Pineapple Cream Pie

Corsican Pebronata de Boeuf

Despite French and Italian influences, the cuisine of the Mediterranean island of Corsica is individualistic. Among its traditional dishes are a number of hearty well seasoned stews. One of the best, *pebronata*, is made in large quantity and can be prepared beforehand and reheated. This is a good buffet dish.

2 large onions, peeled and chopped
3-4 medium-sized garlic cloves, crushed
2/3 cup olive or vegetable oil
2 bay leaves, crumbled
1 teaspoon dried thyme
salt, pepper to taste
5 pounds boneless lean beef (rump, chuck, top or bottom round), cut into 1½-inch cubes
1/4 cup flour
2 cups (about) dry red wine
2 teaspoons (about) ground red peppers or hot sauce
1 cup tomato sauce
1 teaspoon dried oregano

Sauté the onions and garlic in the oil in a large kettle until the onions are tender. Add the bay leaves, thyme, salt and pepper; cook 1 minute. Push aside and add the beef cubes, wiped dry, several at a time, to brown on all sides. Sprinkle with the flour and mix well. Add the wine, cover and cook slowly for 1 hour. Add the red peppers, varying the amount according to taste, tomato sauce, oregano and more wine, if needed. Continue to cook slowly for another 30 minutes, or until the meat is tender. The final sauce should be quite thick. Serves 12.

MENU

Corsican Pebronata de Boeuf
Hot Cooked Macaroni
French Bread
Escarole Salad
Peaches in White Wine

Osso Bucco Milanese

This well-known specialty from Milan, Italy, means "hollow bones." One of the delights in eating the bones or shanks is to extract the marrow with a spoon. A combination of chopped garlic, parsley and grated lemon peel called *gremolata*, is important to this dish. It is a good dish for a company sit-down dinner.

8 meaty veal shanks or shins with marrow in the bones,
cut into 2½-inch pieces
flour
salt, pepper to taste
1/3 cup (about) butter, olive or vegetable oil
1 cup chopped onion
2 large garlic cloves, crushed
1 cup dry white wine
1½ cups canned Italian plum tomatoes,
drained and chopped
1/2 cup (about) beef broth or bouillon
***bouquet garni* (1 bay leaf, 1/2 teaspoon dried thyme,**
2 parsley sprigs)
1 tablespoon grated lemon peel
3 tablespoons chopped fresh parsley

Wipe the veal shanks or shins dry and dust with the flour seasoned with salt and pepper. Heat the butter or oil in a heavy kettle or casserole and brown the meat pieces, a few at a time, on all sides. As they are cooked, transfer to a platter. Sauté the onion and 1 garlic clove in the drippings until tender, adding more butter if needed. Arrange the shanks to stand upright over the onions. Add the wine, tomatoes, broth or bouillon, and *bouquet garni*. Bring to a boil. Reduce the heat, cover and cook slowly for 1½ to 2 hours, until the meat is tender. Add a little more broth during the cooking, if needed. When the cooking is finished, combine the remaining garlic clove, the lemon peel and parsley, and sprinkle over the ingredients. Correct the seasoning and remove and discard the bay leaf and parsley. Serves 6.

MENU

Osso Bucco Milanese
Risotto Milanese or Buttered Rice
Hearts of Lettuce Salad
Bread Sticks
Lemon Sherbet with Chocolate Shavings

Swiss Berner Platte

This national Swiss favorite, named for the charming capital of Berne, is a fascinating, large platter of sauerkraut and a wide variety of meats with vegetable accompaniments. It is fun to serve for an informal sit-down dinner or late supper.

2 pounds sauerkraut
2 tablespoons bacon or pork fat
2 medium-sized onions, peeled and chopped
8 peppercorns
10 juniper berries
salt to taste
2½ cups dry white wine
1/2 pound bacon in one piece
6 smoked pork chops

1 pound pork sausage links, cooked and drained
6 bratwurst or knockwurst, braised and drained
6 thick slices cooked ham
3 cups cooked and drained hot green beans
3 tablespoons butter or margarine
1 garlic clove, minced
pepper to taste
6 medium-sized potatoes, boiled, drained and peeled

Rinse the sauerkraut and drain well to remove all the liquid. Heat the fat in a large kettle. Add the onions and sauté until tender. Add the sauerkraut and sauté about 5 minutes, mixing with a fork. Add the peppercorns, juniper berries, salt, wine and bacon. Cover and cook slowly for 1 hour. Add the pork chops, sausage, bratwurst and ham and continue cooking for another 30 minutes longer, or until all the ingredients are cooked. Remove and discard the peppercorns and juniper berries. Combine the hot green beans, butter and garlic and season with salt and pepper. To serve, spoon the sauerkraut onto a large platter and surround with the meats. Put the potatoes in a bowl and the green beans in another dish; serve with the *platte*. Serves 6.

MENU

Swiss Berner Platte
Hard Rolls
Apple Tarts or Pie

Carbonnade à la Flamande

A beef and onion stew flavored with beer, brown sugar and herbs is traditional fare in Belgium's northern region of Flanders. The name is believed to have derived from the French word for carbon which means broiled or grilled over coals or charcoal.

**3 pounds lean boneless beef chuck or round steak, cut
into 2-inch strips
flour
salt, pepper to taste
1/2 cup lard or butter
4 large onions, peeled and thinly sliced
1-2 garlic cloves, crushed
bouquet garni (1 bay leaf, 1/2 teaspoon crumbled dried
thyme, 4 sprigs fresh parsley, all wrapped in cheesecloth)
2 tablespoons brown sugar
2½ cups (about) light beer
2 tablespoons red wine vinegar
12 boiled medium-sized potatoes
3 tablespoons chopped fresh parsley**

Wipe the meat dry and dredge each strip with flour seasoned with salt and pepper. Set aside. Heat the lard or butter
in a kettle and sauté the onions and garlic in it until tender.
Push aside and add the meat, several strips at a time. Brown
on all sides. Tie the bay leaf, thyme and parsley in a small
square of cheesecloth to make a *bouquet garni*. Add to the
ingredients. Mix in the sugar and beer. Season with salt and
pepper. Cover and cook over low heat about 1½ hours or
until the meat is tender. Add more beer while cooking, if
needed. (The liquid should cover the ingredients while cooking.) Remove and discard the *bouquet garni*. Stir in the vinegar
just before serving. Serve the hot boiled potatoes, garnished
with the parsley, with the stew. Serves 8.

MENU

Carbonnade à la Flamande
Endive Salad
Warm Dinner Rolls
Apricot Tart

Pacific Seafood Stew

This American stew includes a number of seafood treasures that are taken from the Pacific Ocean. It is a good luncheon or supper dish.

1/3 cup vegetable oil
1 large onion, peeled and chopped
1-2 medium-sized garlic cloves, crushed
2 tablespoons tomato paste
2 cups fish broth, bottled clam broth or water
2 cups (about) dry white wine
1 medium-sized bay leaf
1/2 teaspoon dried basil or thyme
3 parsley sprigs
salt, pepper to taste
1 quart hard-shell clams, washed and scrubbed well
1 pound halibut, cut into 2-inch pieces*
1 pound salmon, cut into 2-inch pieces
1 pound lump crabmeat, cleaned
1/4 cup chopped fresh parsley

Heat the oil in a large kettle and sauté the onions and garlic in it until tender. Stir in the tomato paste. Add the broth, wine, bay leaf, basil or thyme, parsley sprigs, salt or pepper and bring to a boil. Lower the heat and cook slowly, covered, for 30 minutes. Add the clams, halibut, salmon and crabmeat and more wine, if desired. Cover and continue to cook slowly about 12 minutes or until the clams have opened and the fish is tender. Remove and discard the bay leaf and parsley sprigs. Add the chopped parsley. Serves 6.
*An equivalent amount of any other kind of white-fleshed fish can be substituted for the halibut, if desired.

MENU

Pacific Seafood Stew
Warm Sourdough Bread

Romaine Lettuce Salad
Blackberry Pie

Coq au Vin

This popular dish, whose French name means simply *chicken in wine*, is made in several variations, but generally includes small white onions and mushrooms. It is a good dish for a Saturday night dinner.

2 frying chickens, about 2½ pounds each, cut up
salt, pepper to taste
10 tablespoons butter or margarine
4 tablespoons (about) olive oil
1 medium-sized piece lean bacon, diced
3 pounds small white onions, peeled
1½ pounds fresh mushrooms, cleaned
1/2 cup brandy
4 cups dry red wine
1/2 teaspoon dried thyme
2 bay leaves
4 parsley sprigs
4 medium-sized garlic cloves, crushed
1/4 cup flour
1/3 cup chopped fresh parsley

Wash the chicken and pat dry. Season with salt and pepper. Set aside. Heat 6 tablespoons of the butter, the oil and the bacon in a large kettle or casserole. Add the onions and sauté about 10 minutes or less, depending on their size. Remove the onions with a slotted spoon and set aside. Add the mushrooms to the drippings and sauté 5 minutes, adding more oil if needed. Remove and set aside. Add the chicken pieces to the drippings and fry until golden on all sides. Pour in the brandy and ignite it. Let burn, shaking the pan, until the flames subside. Return the onions to the kettle. Add the wine, thyme, bay leaves, parsley and garlic. Season with salt and pepper. Bring to a boil. Lower the heat, cover and cook slowly, about

30 minutes or until the chicken is tender. Add the mushrooms during the last 5 minutes of cooking. Blend together 4 tablespoons of softened butter and the flour. Shape into tiny balls and add to the liquid. Stir with a whisk or spoon until well blended. Arrange the chicken, onions and mushrooms on a platter. Cover with the sauce. Garnish with the parsley. Serves 8.

MENU

Coq au Vin
Parsley Potatoes
Hearts of Lettuce Salad
French Bread
Fresh Strawberries and Cream

Hungarian Szekely Goulash

Over the years several variations of Hungary's national stew, *gulyás*, have emerged. One of the best includes sauerkraut and is sometimes called Transylvanian goulash, having been named for a region which is now a part of Rumania. It is a good winter dinner or supper dish.

3 pounds boneless lean pork (or a mixture of 1 pound
boneless beef chuck, 1 pound boneless veal and
1 pound boneless lean pork), cut into 1½-inch cubes
2 tablespoons (about) lard or other fat
2 large onions, peeled and sliced thinly
2 tablespoons paprika
1½ teaspoons caraway seeds
salt, pepper to taste
3 pounds sauerkraut, drained and rinsed
2 cups sour cream at room temperature
1 pound thin egg noodles, cooked and drained (optional)
3 tablespoons butter or margarine (optional)

Cut any fat from the meat and discard it. Brown the meat

in the lard in a large kettle, adding about 1 pound at a time. Remove to a plate after it is browned. Add the onion slices to the kettle, as well as more lard, if needed, and sauté until tender. Stir in the paprika and cook 1 minute. Return the meat to the kettle. Add the caraway seeds, salt, pepper and enough water to cover the ingredients. Cook slowly, covered, for 1 hour. Add the sauerkraut and more water, if needed, and continue to cook slowly about 30 minutes longer or until the meat is tender. Mix in the sour cream and leave on the stove just long enough to heat through. Serve with the noodles, mixed with the butter, if desired. Serves 8.

MENU

Hungarian Szekely Goulash
Hot Buttered Noodles
Rye Bread
Sliced Cucumber Salad
Nut Cake

Carbonada Criolla

South Americans are fond of this flavorful meat and fruit stew, which is sometimes baked and served in a large pumpkin instead of a kettle. It is a good winter dinner dish.

1/4 cup vegetable oil
1 large onion, peeled and chopped
1 garlic clove, crushed
2 pounds stew beef, cut into 1½-inch cubes
1 can (1 pound) tomatoes
1 bay leaf
1/2 teaspoon dried oregano
salt, pepper to taste
1 cup beef broth or bouillon
1 pound sweet potatoes, peeled and cubed
2 cups cubed butternut or acorn squash
1 large green pepper, cleaned and cut into strips

1 cup fresh or frozen corn niblets
1 cup diced fresh or canned peaches
1 medium-sized tart apple, pared, cored and diced

Heat the oil in a large kettle. Add the onions and garlic and sauté until tender. Push aside and add the beef cubes, several at a time, and brown on all sides. Remove to a plate if necessary. Add the tomatoes, bay leaf, oregano, salt and pepper; cook 1 minute. Pour in the broth and bring to a boil. Lower the heat and cook slowly, covered, for 1 hour. Add the sweet potatoes and squash and continue the cooking another 25 minutes or until the vegetables are just tender. Add the green pepper, corn, peaches and apple. Cook 5 minutes longer, or until the ingredients are tender. Serves 6.

MENU

Carbonada Criolla
Warm Cornbread
Strawberry Chiffon Pie

Viennese Chicken Paprikás

A superb chicken stew that probably had its origins in the kitchens of Hungary, chicken paprikás has long been popular fare in Vienna also. It is a good weekend luncheon dish.

2 frying chickens, about 2½ pounds each, cut up
salt, pepper to taste
1/3 cup (about) butter or margarine
2 large onions, peeled and sliced thinly
1-2 tablespoons paprika
2 large tomatoes, peeled and chopped
1 cup (about) chicken broth
2 tablespoons flour
2 cups heavy sweet cream or sour cream
at room temperature

Wash and pat dry the chicken pieces. Season with salt and pepper. Heat the butter in a kettle and brown the chicken, a few pieces at a time, on both sides over moderate heat. Remove from the kettle with tongs and keep warm. Add the sliced onions to the drippings and more butter, if needed. Sauté until tender. Stir in the paprika and cook 1 minute. Add the tomatoes and sauté until mushy, 1 or 2 minutes. Return the chicken pieces to the kettle. Add the broth. Cover and cook slowly for about 30 minutes or until the chicken is just tender. Add more broth while cooking, if needed. Remove the chicken pieces with tongs and keep warm. Scrape the drippings and stir in the flour. Gradually add the cream and cook, stirring, until thickened and smooth. Correct the seasoning. Add the chicken pieces, and leave on the stove long enough to warm through. Garnish the top with chopped fresh dill, if desired. Serves 6 to 8.

MENU

Viennese Chicken Paprikás
Buttered Noodles
Caraway-Flavored Cabbage Salad
Warm Poppy-Seed Rolls
Mocha Torte

Spanish Cocido

This hearty Spanish national stew is made in several regional variations. Always included in it are chickpeas (garbanzos), nutty flavored legumes, and a variety of vegetables and meats. This is a southern version that includes such typical foods as rice, tomatoes and green beans. The stew can be served in three courses: first, the broth, then, the vegetables, and lastly, the meats. This is a good buffet dish.

2 large onions, peeled and chopped
1/3 cup olive or vegetable oil
2 pounds stewing beef (rump, chuck, bottom or top round),

cut into 2-inch cubes
4 pounds beef soup bones with marrow
1/2 pound bacon in one piece
16 cups water
salt, pepper to taste
2 large carrots, scraped and diced
2 cans (1 pound, 4 ounces each) chickpeas, drained
6 large tomatoes, peeled and chopped
1½ cups uncooked rice
2 pounds Spanish sausages *(chorizo)* or
garlic sausages, sliced thinly
red pepper to taste
4 cups frozen green beans
pinch of saffron (optional)

Sauté the onions in the olive oil in a large kettle until tender. Push aside and add the beef cubes, a few at a time, and brown on all sides. Add the beef bones, bacon, water, salt and pepper. Bring to a boil. Lower the heat and cook slowly, covered, for 1 hour. Remove the cover and skim off any fat that has accumulated on the top. Add the carrots and cook 15 minutes. Stir in the chickpeas, tomatoes, rice, sausages and red pepper. Continue to cook about 20 minutes longer or until the ingredients are tender. Add the frozen beans 10 minutes before the cooking is finished. Stir in the saffron before removing from the heat. Remove the bones and take out any marrow left in them. Return the marrow to the stew and discard the bones. Serves 12.

MENU

Spanish Cocido
Warm Cornbread
Baked Custard

Balkan Veal-Barley Stew

Two very nourishing and appealing foods, barley and veal, are combined with seasonings and green beans to make this stew. It is a good Sunday supper dish.

4 pounds veal breast, cut into 2-inch pieces
4 tablespoons vegetable oil
1 large onion, peeled and chopped
2 medium-sized garlic cloves, crushed
salt, pepper to taste
1/2 teaspoon sugar
2 tablespoons all-purpose flour
4 cups beef bouillon
1 can (6 ounces) tomato paste
bouquet garni **(1 bay leaf, 1/2 teaspoon dried thyme,**
2 parsley sprigs)
1 cup pearl barley
3 cups frozen cut-up green beans
1 tablespoon chopped fresh dill

Wipe the veal pieces dry. Heat 2 tablespoons of the oil in a large kettle. Add about half the veal and brown on all sides. Remove to a plate. Add the remaining 2 tablespoons of oil and the veal and brown. Remove also to the plate. Add the onion and garlic to the drippings in the kettle and sauté until tender. Return the veal pieces to the kettle. Season with salt and pepper. Add the sugar and sprinkle with the flour. Stir about so the flour is evenly distributed. Combine the bouillon and tomato paste and pour into the kettle. Add the *bouquet garni*. Bring to a boil. Lower the heat, cover and cook very slowly for 1 hour. Add the barley and continue cooking until it is tender, 45 minutes to 1 hour. Add the green beans 15 minutes before the cooking is finished. Stir in the dill. Remove and discard the bay leaf and parsley. Serves 8.

MENU

Balkan Veal-Barley Stew
Crusty Dark Bread
Yogurt-Cucumber Salad
Cooked Pear Compote

Rabbit Stew Provençale

Europeans, particularly the French, are fond of rich stews featuring hare or rabbit. One of the best is native to Provence and features such favorite foods as tomatoes, mushrooms, olives and herbs.

1 fresh or frozen rabbit, about 3 pounds, cut up
1/3 cup olive or vegetable oil
2 tablespoons butter or margarine
20 small white onions, peeled
2 garlic cloves, crushed
3 medium-sized tomatoes, peeled and chopped
1 bay leaf
1/2 teaspoon dried thyme
1/4 cup brandy (optional)
dry red or white wine
salt, pepper to taste
20 medium-sized fresh mushrooms, cleaned
20 pitted black olives
3 tablespoons chopped fresh parsley

Wash the rabbit pieces and wipe dry. Sauté in the oil and butter in a large kettle until golden on all sides. With tongs remove to a plate. To the drippings add the onions and sauté until tender. Add the garlic, tomatoes, bay leaf, thyme and brandy. Cook 2 minutes. Return the rabbit pieces to the kettle. Cover with wine and season with salt and pepper. Cook slowly, covered, about 30 minutes, or until the rabbit is tender. Add the mushrooms and olives after the dish has been cooking 20 minutes. Stir in the parsley just before serving. Serves 4.

MENU

Rabbit Stew Provençale
Parsley Boiled Potatoes

Beet Salad
Crusty French Bread
Cheese Plate

Polish Bigos

A very old and traditional Polish dish is *bigos* or hunters' stew. Originally it was made with vegetables such as cabbage, onions and mushrooms, apples and prunes, and an abundance of leftover cooked meats and game. Made in great quantity, *bigos* was featured at national holiday meals and parties following the customary hunts. Today this stew is made in many variations, generally with whatever ingredients are on hand. This version is a good buffet dish.

2 ounces dried brown mushrooms
1/4 pound salt pork or bacon, chopped
3 large onions, peeled and sliced thinly
1/2 pound (about 2½ cups) shredded cabbage
1 pound lean beef (chuck, rump, bottom or top round),
cut into 1½-inch cubes
1 pound lean pork, cut into 1½-inch cubes
3 pounds sauerkraut, washed and drained
3 medium-sized tart apples, peeled, cored and chopped
1 can (14½ ounces) whole tomatoes, undrained
1 cup vegetable broth or water
2 teaspoons sugar
2 teaspoons prepared sharp mustard
salt, pepper to taste
1 pound smoked Polish sausage or *kielbasa*, cut into
1-inch rounds
1/2 cup Madeira wine
12 medium-sized potatoes, washed and peeled
1/4 cup chopped fresh parsley

Soak the mushrooms in lukewarm water in a small bowl for 20 minutes. Drain, reserving the mushroom liquid. Press the mushrooms to release all the liquid. Chop and set aside. Put the chopped pork or bacon and sliced onions in a large kettle and sauté until tender. Add the cabbage and sauté about 3 minutes. Push aside and add the beef and pork cubes; brown on all sides. Mix the ingredients together in the kettle. Add the sauerkraut, apples, tomatoes, chopped mushrooms, reserved mushroom liquid, vegetable broth, sugar, mustard, salt and pepper. Cover and cook slowly for about 2 hours. Add the sausage during the last 1/2 hour of cooking. Stir in the Madeira just before removing from the heat. During the last stages of the cooking, boil the potatoes until just tender, and add to the stew or serve separately, sprinkled with the parsley. Serves 12.

Note: Substitute 1 cup sliced fresh or canned mushrooms for the dried ones, if desired.

MENU

Polish Bigos
Pumpernickel
Honey Cake

Chili Con Carne

Controversies rage over the proper ingredients and preparation of this well-known dish. Some enthusiasts include beans with the beef, tomatoes and chili peppers. Others do not. Seasonings vary considerably. There are those who advocate using only chili powder, and those who favor the addition of cayenne, oregano, cumin or garlic. This recipe is my favorite version. It can be made as spicy as the cook desires. It is a good weekday supper dish.

1 pound pinto beans
salt to taste
2 cups chopped onions
2 medium-sized garlic cloves, crushed
3 tablespoons (about) vegetable oil
2 pounds lean round or chuck beef, cut into 1½-inch cubes

1 can (1 pound, 12 ounces each) tomatoes, undrained
1-2 tablespoons chili powder
1/2 teaspoon ground cumin
1 teaspoon ground oregano
1/2 teaspoon crushed red peppers or cayenne
black pepper to taste

Put the beans in a large kettle or pot and cover with water. Leave to soak overnight or for about 9 hours. Bring the beans to a boil. Season with salt. Lower the heat and cook slowly, covered, until the beans are just tender, about 1¼ hours. Do not overcook. Add more water while cooking, if needed. Drain and set aside. Sauté the onions and garlic in the oil in a large kettle until tender. Push aside and add the meat cubes, about 1/2 pound at a time, and brown on all sides. Add more oil, if needed. Stir in the tomatoes and break them up with a spoon. Cook a few minutes, stirring, until the foods are well mixed. Add the remaining ingredients, cover and cook slowly for about 2 hours or until the meat is tender. Add the drained beans during the last 15 minutes of cooking. Serves 8.

MENU

Chili Con Carne
Hot Buttered Rice
Mixed Green Salad
Warm Tortillas
Orange Ambrosia

Curried Chicken From Thailand

Some of the best dishes to be found in the cuisines of Southeast Asian countries are those flavored with curry, a combination of several spices prepared in powder or paste form. The curries of Thailand, which are generally very hot and pungent, are so varied that they even have an intriguing range of colors made by blending various spices, herbs, condiments or other flavorings. The curry used for chicken

is deep yellow and is made by combining turmeric, cardamom, coriander, nutmeg and chilies, among other spices,
with a strong fish sauce. Unfortunately it is not easy to dupli-
cate these curries in an American home as the necessary
native ingredients and implements are not available. This
curry is an adaptation of the Thai version.

3 cups coconut milk
2 tablespoons curry paste
1 cup minced green onions, with tops
2 garlic cloves, crushed
1/3 cup peanut or vegetable oil
2 frying chickens, about 2½ pounds, cut up
1 teaspoon fresh lemon juice
8 cups hot boiled rice
condiments: grated coconut, crumbled cooked bacon,
sliced bananas, chutney, chopped green onions,
peanuts, pickles and green pepper

Prepare the coconut milk and curry paste with the recipes
that follow. To make the curry, sauté the onions and garlic in
the oil in a frying pan or kettle. Add 2 tablespoons of the
curry paste and cook 1 minute. Add the chicken pieces,
and more oil if necessary, and sauté on all sides until golden.
Add the lemon juice and coconut milk and bring to a boil.
Lower the heat, cover and cook slowly for about 35 minutes,
or until the chicken is tender and the sauce is thickened.
Serve with the rice and condiments, each in a separate small
bowl. Serves 8.
*Note: An easier but less flavorful version of this dish can be made
by substituting curry powder for the curry paste.*

Coconut Milk

Put 3 cups freshly grated or packaged or frozen unsweetened coconut and 3 cups of hot water in a bowl and leave for
10 minutes. Strain the liquid from the coconut, discarding
the coconut. Use the "milk" as directed in the recipe.

Curry Paste

Combine 1 tablespoon ground coriander, 1 tablespoon turmeric, 1 teaspoon ground cumin, 1/2 teaspoon ground cardamom, 1/2 teaspoon chili powder and 1/2 teaspoon black pepper in a mortar or bowl and mix with a pestle or spoon to thoroughly combine. Add 2 tablespoons vinegar and 2 tablespoons anchovy paste and mix well. Makes 1/4 cup. (Save the leftover paste for another recipe.)

MENU

Curried Chicken From Thailand
Tossed Green Salad
Pineapple Sherbet with Crushed Pineapple

Israeli Beef Cholent

This traditional Jewish meal-in-one-dish of Central European origin has long been prepared for the Sabbath meals when cooking is forbidden. The name is believed to have derived from the French word *chaud*, warm. It is an excellent supper dish.

1/2 pound dried lima beans
2 medium-sized onions, peeled and sliced
2 large carrots, scraped and sliced
3 tablespoons chicken fat or shortening
1/2 cup pearl barley
8 medium-sized potatoes, pared
2½-3 pounds brisket of beef
3 tablespoons brown sugar
salt, pepper to taste

Soak the beans in water to cover overnight or for about 9 hours. Sauté the onions and carrots in the fat in a large kettle for 5 minutes. Drain the beans and add them, the barley and potatoes. Push the ingredients aside and place the beef in the center. Cover with water and add the sugar, salt and pepper. Cover tightly and cook very slowly on top of the stove for about 2½ hours, or until the meat is tender. During the cooking shake the kettle occasionally to prevent the ingredients from sticking. Serves 8.

MENU

Israeli Beef Cholent
Sliced Tomato Salad
Dark Bread
Stewed Apricots with Cream

Navarin Printanier

Lamb stew prepared with a variety of spring vegetables is as attractive as it is delectable. In France it is made with fresh, tender and young vegetables, but it can also be prepared with frozen ones. Although generally baked in the oven, this dish also can be cooked on top of the stove. It is an excellent dish for a company dinner.

3 pounds lean lamb shoulder, cut into 2-inch cubes
3 tablespoons (about) butter or vegetable oil
1 tablespoon sugar
salt, pepper to taste
2 tablespoons flour
2 cups lamb or beef stock or bouillon
4 medium-sized tomatoes, peeled, seeded and chopped
2 garlic cloves, crushed
1 large bay leaf
1/4 teaspoon dried thyme
6 medium-sized carrots, scraped and cut into
1½-inch lengths
6 small turnips, peeled and cubed
12 small new potatoes or 6 medium-sized ones,

peeled and cut up
16 small white onions, peeled
1 cup shelled fresh or frozen green peas
1 cup cut-up fresh or frozen green beans

Wipe the lamb pieces dry and brown on all sides in the heated butter or oil in a large kettle. Add the sugar and leave over moderately high heat until it caramelizes, about 5 minutes. Season with salt and pepper and sprinkle the flour over the meat. Mix well. Pour in the stock or bouillon and add the tomatoes, garlic, bay leaf and thyme. Mix and bring to a boil. Lower the heat, cover and cook slowly for 1 hour. Take off the stove and spoon the meat onto a plate. Strain the sauce into a bowl. Wash the kettle in which the meat was cooked, and return the strained sauce to it. Add the carrots, turnips, potatoes and onions. Cover and cook slowly until the vegetables are just tender, about 25 minutes. Add the peas and green beans and cook about another 10 minutes, or until tender. (If frozen vegetables are used, add them during the last 5 minutes of cooking.) To serve, arrange the ingredients on a large platter. Serves 8.

MENU

Navarin Printanier
Romaine Salad
Crusty French Bread
Orange or Pineapple Bavarian Cream

Portuguese Seafood Stew

In the villages along the Portuguese Atlantic coast, a favorite dish is *caldeirada*, made with a mélange of fruits from the sea. Fishermen combine the daily catch, perhaps cod, hake, clams, bream, red snapper, squid, crabs, mussels, eel and shrimp, with a few vegetables and seasonings to make a thick and flavorful stew.

3 pounds mixed fish and shellfish, cleaned
3 large onions, peeled and sliced
1-2 garlic cloves, crushed
1/3 cup olive or vegetable oil
3 large tomatoes, peeled and chopped
6 medium-sized potatoes, peeled and sliced thinly
1/2 cup chopped fresh coriander or parsley
salt, pepper to taste
1 cup dry white wine

If the fish is small, leave it whole; otherwise, cut it into serving pieces. Clean the clams and crabs, if used, and crack any shellfish. Sauté the onions and garlic in the oil in a large kettle until tender. Add the tomatoes and cook slowly for 5 minutes. Put the fish, shellfish and potatoes in layers in the kettle. Add the coriander, salt, pepper and wine. Cook slowly until the ingredients are tender, 25 minutes or longer. Serves 8.

MENU

Portuguese Seafood Stew
Cold Cooked Leeks Vinaigrette
Crusty White Bread
Sliced Pineapple au Rhum

Caribbean Chicken Sancocho

In the Spanish-speaking Caribbean islands a popular stew is *sancocho*, made with a variety of meats and vegetables. Most often such favorite foods as yams, dasheens, cassavas, plantains, pineapples and coconuts are among the ingredients. The resulting flavor is most appealing. This version, made with food generally available in the United States, is a good summer buffet dish.

1 pound boneless pork or ham, cut into small cubes
1/2 pound salt pork, diced

1/4 cup (about) vegetable oil
2 frying chickens, about 2½ pounds each, cut up
2 large onions, peeled and sliced
2 garlic cloves, crushed
4 medium-sized tomatoes, peeled, seeded and chopped
2 cups chicken broth
1 bay leaf
1/2 teaspoon dried oregano
3 parsley sprigs
salt, pepper to taste
2 pounds sweet potatoes, peeled and cubed
4 medium-sized carrots, scraped and cut into 1½-inch pieces
2 pounds yellow squash, washed, stemmed and cubed
1/4 cup chopped fresh coriander or parsley

Put the pork or ham, salt pork and oil in a large kettle and sauté until most of the fat is released from the salt pork. Push aside or remove from the kettle. Dry the chicken pieces and sauté a few at a time until golden. Add more oil, if needed. Remove with tongs to a plate. Add the onions and garlic to the drippings and sauté until tender. Add the tomatoes and cook 1 minute. Return the meat and chicken pieces to the kettle. Add the broth, bay leaf, oregano, parsley, salt and pepper and bring to a boil. Lower the heat, cover and cook slowly for 15 minutes. Add the sweet potatoes and carrots. Cook another 15 minutes and add the squash. Continue cooking about 20 minutes longer or until the ingredients are tender. Mix in the coriander. Remove and discard the bay leaf before serving. Serves 10.

MENU

Caribbean Chicken Sancocho
Orange-Cucumber Salad
Warm Corn Muffins
Pineapple Sherbet
Macaroons

French Boeuf Bourguignon

This famous beef stew is cooked *à la bourguignonne*, or "in the style of Burgundy," one of France's great wine producing regions. It is richly flavored with wine and includes small white onions and whole mushrooms, as well as superb garnishes.

5 pounds boneless stewing beef, (chuck, rump, top or bottom round), cut into 1½-inch cubes
1/2 cup diced bacon or salt pork
6 tablespoons (about) olive or vegetable oil
2 carrots, scraped and diced
2 medium-sized onions, peeled and chopped
3 tablespoons flour
3-4 garlic cloves, crushed
2 bay leaves
4 parsley sprigs
1 teaspoon dried thyme
3 cups (about) dry red wine
2 cups beef stock or bouillon
salt, pepper to taste
24 small white onions, peeled
6 tablespoons (about) butter or margarine
24 fresh mushrooms, cleaned
2 tablespoons tomato paste

Dry the beef cubes. Heat the bacon or pork and oil in a large kettle and add the beef, a few cubes at a time, to brown on all sides. Remove to a plate. Add the carrots and onions to the drippings and sauté for 5 minutes. Return the beef to the kettle. Sprinkle with the flour and mix. Add the garlic, bay leaves, parsley, thyme, wine and stock. Season with salt and pepper. Bring to a boil. Lower the heat, cover and cook slowly for about 2 hours or until the meat is tender. Add more wine during the cooking, if needed, but there should not be too much liquid. While the stew is cooking, sauté the onions in 3 tablespoons of butter in a saucepan until golden, a minute or two. Add water to cover and cook, covered, until just tender, about 12 minutes. Cut the mushrooms in half lengthwise and sauté in the remaining butter, adding more if needed, in a skillet for 4 minutes. Ten minutes before the stew is finished cooking add the tomato paste and stir well. Add the onions and mushrooms, with the drippings, just before taking the dish off the heat. Serves 12.

MENU

French Boeuf Bourguignon
Mixed Green Salad
Crusty French Bread
French Pastry or Cheese Plate

West African Jollof

In the small West African coastal countries bordering the Atlantic, a typical stew called *jollof* is made with chicken or meat, or both, rice and native hot seasonings. Generally it is prepared in very large quantities and served at such celebrations as weddings and birthdays. This version of *jollof* can be made even spicier with the addition of more red pepper, if desired.

1/2 pound salt pork, diced
3 tablespoons (about) peanut or vegetable oil
1 pound boneless beef chuck or round,
cut into 1½-inch cubes
2 frying chickens, about 2½ pounds each, cut up
3 large onions, peeled and sliced thinly
4 large tomatoes, peeled and chopped
2 large green peppers, cleaned and cut into strips
2 bay leaves
1-2 teaspoons crushed red peppers
1/2 teaspoon dried thyme
salt, pepper to taste
2 cans (6 ounces each) tomato paste

1 cup water
1 tablespoon fresh lemon juice
2 cups chicken broth
2 cups long grain rice

Put the salt pork and oil in a large kettle and cook until most of the fat is released from the pork. Add the beef cubes, a few at a time, and brown on all sides. Remove to a plate or push aside. Dry the chicken pieces and sauté a few at a time until golden on all sides. Add more oil, if needed. With tongs remove to a plate. Add the onions and sauté until tender. Stir in the tomatoes and green peppers, and more oil, if needed, and sauté 2 minutes. Add the bay leaves, red peppers, thyme, salt, pepper, tomato paste, water and lemon juice and mix well. Cook 1 minute. Return the beef and chicken to the kettle and pour in the chicken broth. Bring to a boil. Lower the heat, cover and cook slowly for 30 minutes. Add the rice and continue to cook slowly, covered, for about 30 minutes, or until the chicken is tender and almost all the liquid has been absorbed by the rice. Serves 10.

Note: Traditional accompaniments for the stew are boiled cabbage or spinach.

MENU

West African Jollof
Mixed Green Salad
Dark Bread
Coconut Pie or Cake

Greek Beef Stifado

In Greek restaurants, it is a premeal custom to visit the kitchen and peer into the pots before ordering. Among the aromatic selections, one customarily will find *stifado*, a well-flavored stew that has been slowly simmered for a long time. This is an excellent dish for an outdoor buffet.

1 cup (about) olive or vegetable oil
4 pounds boneless beef chuck or stew meat,
cut into 1-inch cubes
4 pounds small white onions, peeled
1 can (6 ounces) tomato paste
1½ cups dry red wine
3-4 garlic cloves, peeled and halved
2 sticks cinnamon or 1½ tablespoons ground cinnamon
6 whole cloves
2 bay leaves
salt, pepper to taste

Heat 1/2 cup of the oil in a large kettle. Dry the beef cubes and brown a few pieces at a time in the oil, adding more if needed. Take off the heat and set aside. Sauté the onions in the remaining heated oil in a skillet until golden on all sides. Spoon, with the drippings, over the meat. Do not mix together. Combine the tomato paste and red wine and pour over the meat and onions. Add the remaining ingredients. Cook very slowly, tightly covered, 2½ to 3 hours, or until the meat is tender. During the cooking check now and then to see if the meat is sticking to the kettle. If so, add a little water. The final sauce, however, should be quite thick and will be better if cooked very slowly. Discard the garlic, cinnamon sticks, cloves and bay leaves before serving. Serves 12.

MENU

Greek Beef Stifado
Hot Buttered Rice
Sliced Cucumber-Green Pepper Salad
Sesame Seed Bread
Baklava or Fresh Fruit

Moroccan Chicken Tajine

In Morocco any mixture of ingredients cooked in a glazed earthenware casserole called a *tajine* has the same name.

There are many variations, each including exotic native foods. Although this one is traditionally made with pickled lemons that must be prepared several days beforehand, ordinary fresh lemons are used in this recipe. A good dish for a summer luncheon.

1/2 cup (about) olive or vegetable oil
3 medium-sized onions, peeled and sliced thinly
2-3 garlic cloves, crushed
2 teaspoons ground ginger
2 teaspoons powdered coriander
1/4 cup chopped fresh parsley
salt, pepper to taste
2 frying chickens, about 2½ pounds each, cut up
1½ cups chicken broth or water
2 medium-sized lemons, quartered
1 cup pitted green olives

Heat the oil in a large kettle and add the onions and garlic. Sauté until tender. Mix in the spices, parsley, salt and pepper and cook 2-3 minutes. Dry the chicken pieces and add to the spice mixture. Fry a few pieces at a time until golden on all sides, adding more oil, if needed. Add the broth or water, cover and cook slowly for 30 minutes. Mix in the lemons and olives and continue to cook slowly for another 20 minutes or until the ingredients are tender. Serves 6.

MENU

Moroccan Chicken Tajine
Parsley Boiled Potatoes
Sliced Tomatoes
Crusty White Bread
Canned Figs and Vanilla Ice Cream

Kentucky Burgoo

This famous southern stew has long been served traditionally in Kentucky at all important outdoor gatherings.

Originally made with squirrel and chicken, *burgoo* contains a large number of vegetables. It is cooked outdoors in a large iron kettle and served in tin cups.

4 pounds mixed meat (pork, beef, veal and/or lamb) shanks
1 roasting or stewing chicken, about 4 pounds
1 tablespoon salt
pepper to taste
4 medium-sized potatoes, peeled and cubed
3 carrots, scraped and diced
2 large onions, peeled and chopped
2 cups shredded green cabbage
2 cups fresh or frozen corn kernels
3 medium-sized tomatoes, peeled and diced
1 package (10 ounces) frozen lima beans
1 package (10 ounces) frozen whole okra
2 tablespoons Worcestershire sauce
1 cup diced green pepper

Put the meat shanks and chicken in a large kettle and pour in enough water to just cover them. Season with salt and pepper. Lower the heat, cover and cook slowly for 1½ hours or longer, until the chicken and meat are tender. Remove from the kettle and cut all the meat from the bones. Cut the meat into bite-sized pieces and return to the kettle. Discard any skin and bones. Heat to boiling. Lower the heat and add all the vegetables except the frozen ones and green pepper. Cover and cook slowly for 20 minutes. Add the frozen vegetables, Worcestershire sauce and green pepper and continue cooking until the ingredients are tender. Check the seasoning. Serves 16.

MENU

Kentucky Burgoo
Warm Corn Muffins
Chocolate Frosted Pound Cake or Sponge Cake

Poulet en Cocotte

In France chicken is often cooked *en cocotte* or in a casserole.

1 roasting chicken, 3½-4 pounds
salt, pepper to taste
4 sprigs fresh tarragon or 1/2 teaspoon dried tarragon
3 tablespoons (about) butter or margarine
2 tablespoons (about) olive or vegetable oil
16 small white onions, peeled
1/2 cup tomato sauce
bouquet garni **(1 bay leaf, 1/2 teaspoon dried thyme,**
2 parsley sprigs, wrapped in cheesecloth)
16 small new potatoes, peeled
1 pound fresh mushrooms, cleaned
1 package (9 ounces) frozen artichoke hearts

Wash the chicken and pat dry. Season inside and out with salt and pepper. Put the tarragon in the cavity. Truss the chicken. Heat the butter and oil in a heavy casserole. Add the chicken and brown on all sides, turning carefully with two spoons so the skin is not broken. Remove to a platter or pan. Add the onions to the drippings and more butter, if needed, and sauté them for about 5 minutes, until translucent. Stir in the tomato sauce. Return the chicken to the dish and add the *bouquet garni*. Season with salt and pepper. Cover tightly and cook on the top of the stove for about 1 hour or until the chicken is just tender. Add the onions and potatoes after the dish has been cooking for 30 minutes; add the mushrooms and artichokes after cooking 45 minutes. Take off the heat. Remove the chicken from the pan and carve it. Serve surrounded with the vegetables. Serves 4.

MENU

Poulet en Cocotte
Romaine Lettuce Salad
Crusty White Bread
Chocolate or Strawberry Mousse

Persian Lamb-Vegetable Khoreshe

In Persian cookery a *khoreshe* is a stew made with meat or chicken, fresh or dried vegetables, and spices. Sometimes fruits are added. This adaptation is a good dish for a summer dinner.

**1 large eggplant, about 1½ pounds, stemmed and washed
salt
olive or vegetable oil
2 large onions, peeled and sliced
2 pounds boneless lamb, cut into 1-inch cubes
2 large tomatoes, peeled and chopped
2 tablespoons fresh lemon juice
1 teaspoon ground cinnamon
1/2 teaspoon ground nutmeg
pepper to taste**

Slice the unpeeled eggplant and put in a colander or strainer. Sprinkle with salt and leave to drain for 30 minutes. Pat dry and set aside. Heat 1/4 cup of oil in a skillet and sauté the eggplant slices, several at a time, until just tender. Add more oil as needed. As they are cooked, remove them to a plate and set aside. Heat 1/4 cup of oil in a large kettle and add the onions. Sauté until tender. Push aside and add the lamb cubes. Brown on all sides. Cover and cook slowly for 20 minutes. Add the sautéed eggplant, tomatoes, lemon juice, cinnamon and nutmeg. Season with salt and pepper and add 1/2 cup water. Cover and cook slowly for about 1 hour or until the ingredients are cooked. Check occasionally to see if a little more water is needed. Serves 6.

MENU

*Persian Lamb-Vegetable Khoreshe
Buttered Rice
Mixed Green Salad
Crusty Dark Bread
Vanilla Ice Cream with Chopped Fresh Peaches*

Corsican Lamb Stufatu

In Corsica, a lovely French island, there are a number of hearty meat stews, enriched with local seasonings, that are called *stufatus*. This variation also includes macaroni and mushrooms. A good winter dinner dish.

**3 pounds boneless lamb shoulder, cut into
1½-inch cubes
salt, pepper to taste
1/3 cup (about) olive or vegetable oil
2 pounds small white onions, peeled
2-3 garlic cloves, crushed
2 medium-sized tomatoes, peeled and chopped
1½ cups dry white wine
1/2 teaspoon dried basil
8 ounces elbow macaroni or twists
2 cups sliced mushrooms
2 tablespoons butter or margarine
2 tablespoons fresh lemon juice
1/3 cup chopped fresh parsley**

Cut off and discard any excess fat from the lamb. Wipe dry and season with salt and pepper. Heat the oil in a large kettle and brown the lamb, a few pieces at a time, on all sides. Push aside and add the onions and garlic. Sauté until tender. Add the tomatoes, wine and basil. Season with salt and pepper. Bring to a boil. Lower the heat, cover and cook slowly for 1 hour or until the meat and onions are tender. Meanwhile cook the macaroni in boiling salted water until just tender; drain. Sauté the mushrooms in the butter and lemon juice for 3 minutes. Add the mushrooms, macaroni and parsley to the lamb mixture. Cook slowly 5 minutes longer. Serves 8 to 10.

MENU

*Corsican Lamb Stufatu
Artichoke Heart-Lettuce Salad*

Crusty White Bread
Cream Puffs or Eclairs

Sweet-Sour Short Ribs With Noodles

This German-inspired stew is inexpensive and hearty, and makes a good dish for a weekday dinner.

4 pounds beef short ribs, cut into 3-inch pieces
flour
salt, pepper to taste
3 tablespoons shortening or vegetable oil
1 large onion, peeled and sliced
1 cup beef bouillon or water
1/4 cup wine vinegar
3 tablespoons brown sugar
1/2 cup catsup
1/4 cup soy sauce
2 cups fine egg noodles, cooked and drained
1½ cups frozen green peas

Dredge the short ribs with flour seasoned with salt and pepper. Leave on a plate. Heat the shortening in a kettle and sauté the onions in it until tender. Push aside and add the short ribs, a few at a time, to brown on all sides. Pour in the bouillon and bring to a boil. Lower the heat, cover and cook slowly for 1½ hours. Take off the stove and let cool. Skim off any accumulated fat from the top. Add the vinegar, brown sugar, catsup and soy sauce. Mix well. Return to the stove and cook another 30 minutes or until the meat is tender. Mix in the cooked noodles and peas during the last 7 minutes of cooking. Serves 4.

MENU

Sweet-Sour Short Ribs With Noodles
Cabbage-Carrot Salad

Warm Dark Rolls
Baked Apples

Costa Brava Seafood Stew

Zarzuela de mariscos is a very popular stew along the Spanish Mediterranean coast. Its name, which means "musical comedy of seafood," is said to have derived from a seventeenth century performance given at the palace of King Philip IV, La Zarzuela. This particular version is good for a summer lunch.

2 pounds mixed white-fleshed fish (halibut, bass, red snapper, flounder, haddock), cut in chunks
2 small squid, cleaned and cut up
flour
1/2 cup (about) olive oil
24 large shrimp, shelled and deveined
1 large onion, peeled and chopped
1-2 garlic cloves, minced
3 large tomatoes, peeled and chopped
1 bay leaf
salt, pepper to taste
dry white wine
1 can pimiento, chopped
1/3 cup chopped fresh parsley
2 tablespoons brandy or Pernod

Dust the fish and squid with flour. Heat the oil in a kettle and fry the seafood in it on both sides until golden. Remove to a warm platter. Add the shrimp and sauté in the drippings until pink. Add more oil, if needed. Remove to a platter. Add the onion and garlic to the drippings and sauté until tender. Mix in the tomatoes and bay leaf and cook for 2 minutes. Return the fish, squid and shrimp to the kettle. Season with salt and pepper. Add white wine to cover. Cook over moderate heat about 10 minutes, or until the ingredients are tender. Add the pimiento, parsley and brandy. Cook another minute or two. Serves 6.

MENU

Costa Brava Seafood Stew
Buttered Rice
Mixed Green Salad
Crusty White Bread
Fresh Peach Tart

New England Boiled Dinner

Although not exactly a stew in the true sense, this traditional New England one-pot meal has long been a treasured dish. It is easy to prepare and can be reheated.

4-5 pounds corned beef brisket
6 carrots, scraped
6 medium-sized onions, peeled
6 medium-sized potatoes, peeled
2 medium-sized white turnips, pared and quartered
1 head green cabbage, coarsely shredded
6 medium-sized beets, cooked, peeled and kept warm

Wash the beef and put in a kettle. Cover with cold water. Bring to a boil. Lower the heat, cover and cook very slowly for 3-4 hours or until the meat is tender. Add the carrots, onions, potatoes and turnips during the last 30 minutes of cooking. Add the cabbage about 20 minutes before the end of the cooking. To serve, take out the meat and slice. Put in the center of a platter and arrange the cooked vegetables around it. Serve the beets separately. Serves 6.

MENU

New England Boiled Dinner
Warm Parkerhouse Rolls
Apple Pie

Dutch Hutspot

The Dutch version of hotchpotch or thick stew traditionally is made with beef and a few humble vegetables. It is eaten throughout the year but particularly to celebrate the end of the Spanish siege of Leyden in 1574, when the starving population was given *hutspot*. It is a good winter supper dish.

**2 pounds beef chuck or flank
1 teaspoon salt
1½ pounds carrots, scraped and sliced
2 pounds (about 6 medium-sized) potatoes,
peeled and quartered
2 large onions, peeled and chopped
2 tablespoons light cream or milk
2 tablespoons butter or margarine
salt, pepper to taste**

Cut any fat from the beef and, if the flank is used, take off any membranes. Put in a large saucepan with the salt and 4 cups of water. Bring to a boil. Remove any scum that rises to the top. Lower the heat, cover and simmer about 1½ hours. Add the carrots, potatoes and onions and simmer another hour, or until the vegetables are tender. Remove the meat to a warm platter and cut into strips. If flank is used it should be cut across the grain. Take out the vegetables and mash with the cream, butter, salt and pepper. Add some of the broth to thin the mixture, if desired. To serve, spoon the vegetables onto a platter and surround with the meat slices. Serves 6.

MENU

*Dutch Hutspot
Cole Slaw
Warm Dark Rolls
Rice or Berry Pudding*

Spanish Bean-Sausage Stew

This savory stew, called *fabada a la Asturiana*, is one of Spain's great dishes. It is from the northwest region of Asturias along the Bay of Biscay, and its name derives from the local large white bean, *fabe*, a traditional ingredient in the stew. Because the native sausages and pork products are not easily obtainable outside of Spain, this dish is an adaptation of the original.

2 pounds large white beans, washed and drained
6 cups water
3 large onions, peeled and coarsely chopped
3 garlic cloves, crushed
6 tablespoons olive or vegetable oil
2 cans (6 ounces each) tomato paste
salt, pepper to taste
1 pound smoked bacon in one piece
8 smoked ham hocks
1 pound blood sausage (optional)
1 pound *chorizo* (Spanish sausage) or other garlic sausage, sliced and cooked
1/4 teaspoon ground saffron, previously soaked in hot water

Cover the beans with water in a kettle and bring to a boil. Boil for 2 minutes. Remove from the heat. Cover and let stand for 1 hour. Meanwhile, sauté the onions and garlic in the olive oil in a large casserole or heavy kettle until tender. Stir in the tomato paste and season with salt and pepper. When the beans are done, put them, with their liquid, in the casserole or kettle over the onions. Mix well. Add the bacon. Pour in enough water to completely cover the ingredients. Bring to a boil. Lower the heat, cover tightly and cook as slowly as possible for 1 hour. Add the ham hocks and blood sausage and continue cooking slowly for about 1 hour longer or until the ingredients are cooked. Add the *chorizo* and saffron 30 minutes before the dish is finished cooking. Add more water while cooking, if needed. Serves 8 to 10.

MENU

Spanish Bean-Sausage Stew
Warm Corn Bread
Sliced Fresh or Canned Pineapple

Daube de Boeuf

This French country stew takes its name from the earthenware pot, or *daubière*, in which it is cooked. It may also be prepared in a kettle, and makes an excellent dish for company.

**3 pounds lean stewing beef (rump, chuck, top or
bottom round), cut into 2-inch cubes
1 cup dry white or red wine
1/4 cup brandy
1/2 cup olive or vegetable oil
2 large onions, peeled and sliced thinly
4 carrots, scraped and diced
2 bay leaves
1 teaspoon dried thyme
1/4 cup chopped fresh parsley
salt, freshly ground pepper to taste
1/2 cup diced thick bacon
2 garlic cloves, crushed
3 medium-sized tomatoes, peeled, seeded and chopped
1 cup sliced fresh mushrooms
1 small strip orange peel
1/2 teaspoon dried rosemary
12 pitted black olives**

Put the beef cubes, wine, brandy, 1/4 cup olive oil, 1 sliced onion, 2 diced carrots, bay leaves, thyme and 2 tablespoons parsley in a large bowl. Season with salt and pepper; marinate about 2½ hours. Stir the ingredients now and then. When ready to cook, put the bacon, garlic, remaining 2 tablespoons of oil, 1 sliced onion and 2 diced carrots in a kettle and sauté for 5 minutes. Take the meat from the marinade and wipe dry. Reserve the marinade. Brown a few pieces at a time in the oil drippings, pushing the vegetables aside. When all the meat is browned mix in the tomatoes, mushrooms, orange peel and rosemary. Season with salt and pepper. Pour in the reserved marinade, including the vegetables, cover and cook slowly for 1 hour. Stir in the olives after cooking for 30 minutes. When the cooking is finished, add the remaining parsley. Remove and discard the bay leaves. Serves 8 to 10.

MENU

Daube de Boeuf
Boiled Potatoes or Rice
Mixed Green Salad
French Bread
Cheese Plate

San Francisco Cioppino

This marvelous seafood stew is believed to have been created in San Francisco, but nobody knows how it got the name *cioppino*. Some people suspect that Italian or perhaps Portuguese fishermen first prepared *cioppino*, since it resembles stews of the Mediterranean. At any rate, restaurants along Fishermen's Wharf started serving it about 1900, and it has been a treasured specialty in California ever since. This is one of many variations. A good late supper dish.

1 large onion, peeled and chopped
2-3 garlic cloves, crushed
1 medium-sized green pepper, seeded and diced
1/3 cup olive or vegetable oil
2 cans (1 pound each) tomatoes
1 can (8 ounces) tomato sauce
1 bay leaf
1/4 teaspoon dried oregano, thyme, rosemary or basil
or 1/8 teaspoon of two of them

salt, pepper to taste
2 pounds firm fish (bass, halibut, cod, rock, haddock)
1 large Dungeness crab or lobster
1 dozen fresh clams in shells
1 pound large shrimp in shells
2 cups (about) dry white or red wine

Sauté the onion, garlic and green pepper in the oil in a large kettle until tender. Add the tomatoes, tomato sauce, bay leaf, herbs, salt and pepper and bring to a boil. Lower the heat, cover and simmer slowly for 1 hour. While the sauce is cooking, cut the fish into serving pieces. Clean and crack the crab or lobster and put the pieces in a large kettle. Scrub the clams to remove any dirt. Cut the shrimp shells down the backs and remove any black veins. Place the clams and shrimp both over the crabs. Add the fish and then pour the sauce over the seafood. Add the wine. Cover and cook slowly, 20-30 minutes, or until the clams open and the seafood is cooked. Add more wine while cooking, if needed. Discard the bay leaf. Serves 6.

MENU

San Francisco Cioppino
Warm Sourdough or French Bread
Strawberry Ice Cream Pie

South American Estofado

In the various South American cuisines there are several versions of interesting stews called *estofados*. Of European origin, they differ in that the ingredients include such American foods as corn and sweet potatoes.

1 large onion, peeled and chopped
3 tablespoons vegetable oil
2 pounds stew beef, cut into 1½-inch cubes
beef bouillon
salt, pepper to taste

6 small sweet potatoes, peeled
6 medium-sized white potatoes, peeled
4 carrots, scraped
2 cups fresh or frozen corn kernels
1 medium-sized green pepper, seeded and chopped
2 tablespoons chopped fresh parsley
1/8 teaspoon cayenne pepper

Sauté the onion in the oil in a large kettle until tender. Push aside and add the beef, several cubes at a time, to brown on all sides. Add the bouillon to cover, salt and pepper, cover and cook slowly for 1 hour. Add the vegetables, except the green pepper, and more bouillon, if needed. Cook slowly, covered, for about 30 minutes longer, or until the ingredients are cooked. Add the green pepper, parsley and cayenne 5 minutes before the cooking is finished. Serves 8.

MENU

South American Estofado
Sliced Cucumbers and Tomatoes Vinaigrette
Warm Corn Bread
Banana Cream Pie

Moroccan Lamb Couscous

In Morocco and other North African countries, a *couscous* is a favorite hearty stew made with a grain of the same name, vegetables, meat or poultry. The grain is sold in the United States at supermarkets or specialty food stores. Traditionally the stew is cooked in a *couscoussière*, a sort of double boiler with a perforated top pot placed over a kettle.

1 cup chickpeas
1 package (500 grams or 17 ounces) *couscous*
3 pounds lean lamb, leg or shoulder, cut into large cubes
1/3 cup (about) olive or vegetable oil

2 large onions, peeled and chopped
1 can (6 ounces) tomato paste
1 teaspoon ground red pepper
1/2 teaspoon ground cumin
salt, pepper to taste
10 cups water or meat broth
3 carrots, scraped and sliced thickly
2 large zucchini, washed and sliced thickly
2 medium-sized turnips, peeled and cut into large cubes
1 large green pepper, seeded and cut into strips
1/2 cup chopped fresh coriander or parsley

Soak the chickpeas in water to cover overnight. Spread the *couscous* on a large tray or platter and sprinkle with enough water to dampen. Mix about with the hands. Brown the lamb cubes, several pieces at a time, in the oil in a *couscoussière*, soup pan or Dutch oven. Remove to a plate. Add the onions to the drippings and sauté until tender. Stir in the tomato paste, red pepper, cumin, salt and pepper. Add the water or broth and bring to a boil. Return the lamb to the kettle. Add the chickpeas and lower the heat. Cook slowly, covered, for 30 minutes. Add the carrots, zucchini, turnips and green pepper to the stew. Put the *couscous* in the top of the cooker, or in a colander lined with cheesecloth, and place over the kettle. Cover and continue cooking for about 30 minutes longer, or until the *couscous* and stew ingredients are cooked. Stir in the coriander or parsley. To serve, spoon the *couscous* onto a large platter and arrange the lamb and vegetables around it. Sprinkle some of the chickpeas and liquid over the top as a garnish. Serves 8.

Note: Canned chickpeas can be used, if desired. If so, it will not be necessary to soak them overnight.

MENU

Moroccan Lamb Couscous
Fresh Fruit Compote

Country Fish-Vegetable Stew

A nourishing stew that can be easily made with fresh or frozen codfish fillets.

4 medium-sized potatoes, pared and cubed
3 carrots, scraped and sliced
2 cups cut-up green beans
3 medium-sized onions, peeled and quartered
salt, pepper to taste
1½ pounds codfish fillets, cut up
2 tablespoons butter or margarine, softened
2 tablespoons flour
1/3 cup chopped fresh parsley

Put the potatoes, carrots, green beans and onions in a soup pan or Dutch oven. Add enough water to cover them. Season with salt and pepper. Cover and cook slowly for 15 minutes. Add the codfish and a little more water and continue to cook slowly for about 10 minutes or until the ingredients are tender. Combine the softened butter and flour and form into tiny balls. Drop into the stew and cook slowly, stirring, until thickened. Stir in the parsley. Serves 4.

MENU

Country Fish-Vegetable Stew
Buttered Toasted English Muffins
Warm Apple Pie

Grecian Lamb-Artichoke Stew

The Greeks are devoted to a stew made with an interesting combination of lamb and artichokes which is flavored with fresh lemon juice.

1/4 cup olive or vegetable oil
1 large onion, peeled and chopped

3 pounds shoulder of lamb, cut up
2 tablespoons flour
3 cups water
juice of 2 lemons
salt, pepper to taste
2 packages (9 ounces each) frozen artichoke hearts,
defrosted
2 eggs

Heat the oil in a large skillet. Add the onion and sauté until tender. Wipe the lamb dry and brown on all sides in the drippings. Sprinkle with the flour and mix well. Add the water, juice of 1 lemon, salt and pepper and cook slowly, covered, for 45 minutes. Add the artichokes and cook until tender, about 15 minutes. Remove from the heat. Beat the eggs until creamy. Stir in the remaining lemon juice. Slowly add some of the hot stew liquid. Mix well and return to the stew. Cook over low heat, mixing well, until the sauce thickens. Do not boil. Remove from the heat and serve at once. Serves 6 to 8.

MENU

Grecian Lamb-Artichoke Stew
Sesame Seed Bread
Baklava or Honeyed Walnut Cake

Napoleon's Poulet Marengo

This popular dish was created by Napoleon's chef, Dunand, after the French won an outstanding victory against the Austrians in the northern town of Marengo in 1800.

2 frying chickens, about 2½ pounds each, cut up
salt, pepper to taste
6 tablespoons olive oil
3 tablespoons butter or margarine
1 pound fresh mushrooms, cleaned and dried
2 garlic cloves

1 cup chopped onions
1/3 cup tomato purée
1 cup dry white wine
4 medium-sized tomatoes, peeled, seeded, chopped
***bouquet garni* (bay leaf, sprig of parsley,**
1/4 teaspoon thyme)

Wash the chicken pieces and wip dry. Season with salt and pepper. Heat the oil and butter in a large heavy casserole. Add the chicken pieces and fry until golden on all sides. Remove to a warm platter. Carefully pull the stems from one half pound of the mushrooms. Reserve the caps. Slice the stems and the other half pound of mushrooms. Sauté in the drippings for 4 minutes. With a slotted spoon remove to a plate. Add the garlic and onions to the drippings and sauté until tender. Stir in the tomato purée and wine. Bring to a boil. Cook over fairly high heat for 5 minutes. Return the chicken pieces to the kettle. Add the tomatoes, *bouquet garni* and season with salt and pepper. Cook slowly, covered, for about 35 minutes, or until the chicken is tender. Add the reserved sautéed sliced mushrooms and mushroom caps 10 minutes before the cooking is finished. Remove and discard the bay leaf and parsley. To serve, arrange the chicken pieces on a large platter. Spoon the tomato sauce and sliced mushrooms over them. Top with the mushroom caps. Serves 8.

MENU

Napoleon's Poulet Marengo
Buttered Crusty French Bread
French Pastries

Japanese Sukiyaki

This popular Japanese dish is an excellent company meal that can be made in front of guests, in the kitchen or outdoors, if desired. An electric skillet, special sukiyaki pan or ordinary skillet can be used.

1¼ cups soy sauce
1¼ cups *sake* or dry white wine
1/3 cup sugar
1½ teaspoons monosodium glutamate
1 cup (about) vegetable oil
3 pounds beef sirloin, thinly sliced
3 medium-sized onions, peeled and thinly sliced
8 green onions, cut into 3-inch lengths
1/2 pound fresh mushrooms, cleaned and sliced
1 cup sliced bamboo shoots

Combine the soy sauce, *sake*, sugar and monosodium gluta-mate. Pour into a pitcher and set aside. Add enough oil to grease a sukiyaki cooker or skillet. With chopsticks or a fork, dip the meat slices, a few at a time, into the soy-*sake* mixture and spread over the surface of the skillet. Brown and push aside. Add the vegetables, a few at a time, and a generous portion of the soy-*sake* mixture. Cook, turning until just tender. Do not overcook as the vegetables should be just tender or a little crisp. Serves 8.
Note: When cooking in front of guests arrange all the ingredients attractively on bamboo dishes or platters and place near the cooking utensils. Cook slowly, being careful not to overload the utensil with too many ingredients.

MENU

Japanese Sukiyaki
Steamed Rice
Crisp Crackers
Fruit-Topped Lemon Sherbet

Southern Chicken and Okra Stew

A good Sunday dinner dish.

1 frying chicken, about 3 pounds, cut up
3 tablespoons butter or margarine

1 tablespoon olive or vegetable oil
1 large onion, peeled and chopped
2 tablespoons tomato paste
1/2 cup (about) water
1/2 teaspoon dried oregano
salt, pepper to taste
2 packages (10 ounces each) frozen okra, defrosted,
     or fresh okra, if available
juice of 1/2 lemon

Wash the chicken pieces and wipe dry. Melt the butter with the oil in a large skillet and fry the chicken on all sides until golden. Cover and cook over low heat for 15 minutes. Remove the chicken to a plate. Add the onion to the drippings and sauté until tender. Stir in the tomato paste, water, oregano, salt and pepper and mix well. Return the chicken to the kettle. Add the okra. Cook slowly, covered, about 20 minutes, until the chicken and okra are tender. Add a little more water while cooking, if needed. Mix in the lemon juice and serve. Serves 4.

MENU

Southern Chicken and Okra Stew
Warm Corn Sticks
Peach-Vanilla Ice Cream Coupes

Portuguese Pork-Clam Stew

An unusual combination that was created by Portuguese fishermen with their favorite meat and one of their best seafoods.

2 pounds lean boneless pork, cut into small cubes
1/4 cup (about) olive or vegetable oil
2 large onions, peeled and sliced
1-2 garlic cloves, crushed
4 large tomatoes, peeled and chopped

1 can (6 ounces) tomato paste
dry white wine or water
1/2 teaspoon paprika
salt, pepper to taste
24 hard-shelled clams, scrubbed and washed
1/3 cup chopped fresh parsley

Dry the pork cubes and brown on all sides in the oil in a large skillet. Remove with a slotted spoon. Add the onions to the drippings and more oil, if needed, and sauté until tender. Return the pork to the skillet. Add the tomatoes and sauté 2 or 3 minutes. Stir in the tomato paste. Add enough wine or water to cover the ingredients. Mix in the paprika, salt and pepper. Stir well and bring to a boil. Lower the heat and cook slowly, covered, about 1½ hours, or until the meat is tender. Add more wine during the cooking, if needed. Add the clams about 15 minutes before the cooking is finished, or until the shells open. Mix in the parsley. Serves 4.

MENU

Portuguese Pork-Clam Stew
Crusty White Bread
Orange Custard

Hasenpfeffer

This flavorful German specialty, which means "hare pepper," can be made with rabbit, which is often available frozen in supermarkets, or with chicken.

2 fresh or frozen rabbits (2½-3 pounds each),
cut into serving pieces
equal parts of wine vinegar and water to cover the
rabbit pieces
2 medium-sized onions, peeled and sliced
2 bay leaves
4 juniper berries

4 whole cloves
2 tablespoons sugar
6 peppercorns, bruised
salt and pepper to taste
flour
butter or margarine
1/2 cup sour cream at room temperature

Put the rabbit pieces in a large crock or kettle, and add the vinegar, water, onions, bay leaves, juniper berries, cloves, sugar, peppercorns and salt. Let stand, covered, in a cool place for 2 days. Turn over the rabbit pieces 1 or 2 times daily. When the marinating is finished, take out the rabbit pieces and strain the marinade, reserving it. Dry the rabbit pieces, and dust with flour seasoned with salt and pepper. Fry in butter in a kettle until golden on all sides. Add some of the strained marinade and cook very slowly, covered, until the rabbit is tender, about 1 hour. Add more marinade as needed while cooking. Mix in the sour cream and remove from the stove. Serves 6.

MENU

Hasenpfeffer
Crusty Dark Bread
Warm Apple Strudel

Mediterranean Fish Stew

Serve from a handsome tureen for a company supper or late evening meal.

2 medium-sized onions, peeled and sliced
1-2 garlic cloves, crushed
1/3 cup olive or vegetable oil
1 can (29 ounces) tomatoes
1 large bay leaf
1/2 teaspoon dried basil

**3 parsley sprigs
1 cup dry white wine
3 pounds mixed cleaned fish, cut into serving pieces
3 flat anchovy fillets, drained and cut up
pepper to taste
1 pound whole fresh mushrooms, cleaned
3 tablespoons butter or margarine
1 tablespoon fresh lemon juice
1/4 cup chopped fresh parsley
slices of crusty white bread**

Sauté the onions and garlic in the oil in a skillet or large saucepan until tender. Add the tomatoes, bay leaf, basil and parsley and cook 5 minutes. Add the wine, fish, anchovies and pepper. Pour in enough water to cover. Cook over fairly high heat until the fish is just tender, about 12 minutes. While the stew is cooking, sauté the mushrooms in the butter and lemon juice for 5 minutes. Add, with the parsley, to the stew. Correct the seasoning. Discard the bay leaf and parsley sprigs. Spoon the fish, mushrooms and broth over the crusty bread slices in large soup bowls. Serves 6 to 8.

MENU

*Mediterranean Fish Stew
Warm Garlic Bread
Cheese Plate with Crackers*

Pollo alla Cacciatora

Italian chicken cooked in hunter's style, with vegetables, wine and herbs, is a well-known dish that is excellent fare for any dinner.

**2 frying chickens, about 2½ pounds each, cut up
salt, pepper to taste
1/4 cup butter or margarine
3 tablespoons (about) olive or vegetable oil**

3/4 pound fresh mushrooms, cleaned and sliced
2 medium-sized onions, peeled and sliced
1-2 garlic cloves, crushed
1 can (1 pound, 12 ounces) Italian-style tomatoes
1 cup dry white wine
1/2 teaspoon dried thyme
1/2 teaspoon dried oregano
1/4 cup chopped fresh parsley

Wash the chicken pieces and wipe dry. Season with salt and pepper. Heat the butter and oil in a large kettle. Add the chicken and brown on all sides until golden. Remove to a plate. Add the mushrooms to the drippings and sauté for 4 minutes. With a slotted spoon, remove to a plate. Add the onions and garlic and more oil, if needed. Sauté until the onions are tender. Return the chicken pieces to the kettle. Add the tomatoes, wine, thyme, oregano and season with salt and pepper. Bring to a boil. Lower the heat and cook slowly, covered, about 45 minutes, or until the chicken is tender. Stir in the mushrooms and parsley 5 minutes before the cooking is finished. Serves 8.

MENU

Pollo alla Cacciatora
Bread Sticks
Spumoni Ice Cream

New Zealand Lamb Stew

Some of the world's best lamb is from the small country of New Zealand. It is particularly good in this wine-flavored stew enhanced with vegetables.

4 pounds lamb shoulder, cut into large pieces
1/4 cup (about) vegetable oil
2 medium-sized onions, peeled and sliced
1 garlic clove, crushed

2 carrots, scraped and sliced
2 cups dry red wine
1 teaspoon dried oregano or rosemary
salt, pepper to taste
1 package (10 ounces) frozen green peas
1/2 pound sliced fresh mushrooms
or 1 can (6 ounces) sliced mushrooms, drained

Dry the lamb and brown in the oil on all sides in a large kettle. Remove to a platter. Pour off any excess fat. Add the onions, garlic, carrots and more oil to the kettle, if needed. Sauté 5 minutes. Return the lamb to the kettle. Add the wine, oregano, salt and pepper. Bring to a boil. Lower the heat and cook slowly, covered, about 1¼ hours, or until the lamb is cooked. Add the peas and mushrooms 10 minutes before the cooking is finished. Serves 8.

MENU

New Zealand Lamb Stew
Warm Bran Muffins
Strawberry Chiffon Pie

Azerbaidzhan Spinach-Veal Stew

In Russia's southern republic of Azerbaidzhan cooks have long filled stewpots with the highly seasoned favorite foods found in this recipe.

2 pounds veal or lamb shoulder, cut into 1½-inch cubes
2 tablespoons (about) vegetable oil
1 large onion, peeled and sliced
1/2 cup minced green onions, with tops
1 garlic clove, crushed
1/3 cup tomato paste
2 pounds fresh spinach, cleaned and cut up
water
salt, pepper to taste

1 cup plain yogurt at room temperature
1 tablespoon chopped fresh dill

Trim any excess fat from the meat and wipe dry. Brown on all sides in the oil in a skillet or Dutch oven. Push aside and add the onions, garlic and more oil, if needed. Sauté until tender. Stir in the tomato paste and spinach and mix well. Add water to cover, and season with salt and pepper. Bring to a boil. Lower the heat, cover and cook slowly for about 1¼ hours or until the meat is cooked. Add a little more water, if needed, during the cooking. When done, stir in the yogurt and dill and leave on the stove long enough to heat through. Serves 6.

MENU

Azerbaidzhan Spinach-Veal Stew
Crusty Dark Bread
Raisin-Rice Pudding

Chicken-Vegetable Stew with Pasta

A hearty dish good for a winter meal.

1 stalk celery, chopped
1 carrot, peeled and chopped
1 medium-sized onion, peeled and chopped
1/4 cup olive or vegetable oil
1 teaspoon paprika
8 chicken thighs (about 2 pounds)
1 can (1 pound) tomatoes
3 cups cut-up fresh vegetables
1 tablespoon fresh lemon juice
salt, pepper to taste
2 cups pasta (spaghettini, macaroni or noodles)
1/2 cup chopped fresh parsley
1-2 teaspoons seeded and crushed red peppers
(optional)

Sauté the celery, carrot, and onion in the oil in a large skillet until tender. Stir in the paprika and cook 1 minute. Dry the chicken thighs and brown until golden on all sides. Add the tomatoes, vegetables, lemon juice, salt and pepper. Cook slowly, covered, for 30 minutes, or until the chicken is cooked. Meanwhile, cook the pasta and drain. Add, with the parsley and peppers, to the chicken mixture and cook another 5 minutes. Serves 4.

MENU

Chicken-Vegetable Stew with Pasta
Wheat Crackers
Chocolate Ice Cream with Grated Coconut

Budapest Beef Goulash

This is a Hungarian goulash that would be excellent for an evening get-together.

> **2 pounds boneless beef chuck or stew meat,**
> **cut into 1½-inch cubes**
> **2 tablespoons (about) lard or shortening**
> **2 large onions, peeled and chopped**
> **2-3 tablespoons paprika**
> **salt, pepper to taste**
> **2 medium-sized tomatoes, peeled and chopped**
> **1 pound (3 medium-sized) potatoes, peeled and chopped**

Wipe the meat cubes dry. Brown a few pieces at a time on all sides in lard in a skillet or large saucepan. Push aside and add the onions and more lard, if needed. Sauté until tender. Stir in the paprika and cook 1 minute. Season with salt and pepper. Add enough water to cover and cook very slowly, tightly covered, for 1 hour. Add the tomatoes and potatoes. Continue to cook another 30 minutes, or until the beef and potatoes are tender. Add a little more water during the cooking, if needed. Serves 4 to 6.

MENU

Budapest Beef Goulash
Pumpernickel
Chocolate-Garnished Cream Puffs

Lemony Veal Stew

This stew is elegant as a main course.

2 pounds boneless veal, cut into 1½-inch cubes
flour
salt, pepper to taste
2 large carrots, scraped and diced
2 large onions, peeled and chopped
3 tablespoons (about) butter or margarine
4 medium-sized potatoes, peeled and cubed
2 teaspoons grated lemon rind
juice of 2 lemons
pinch of nutmeg

Dry the veal cubes and dredge in flour seasoned with salt and pepper. In a skillet sauté the carrots and onions in the butter for 5 minutes. Push aside, add the floured veal cubes, and brown on all sides. Add more butter, if needed. Add water to cover and cook slowly, covered, for 1½ hours. Add the potatoes and continue to cook slowly for 20 minutes, or until the ingredients are cooked. Add more water during the cooking, if needed. Stir in the lemon rind, lemon juice and nutmeg. Cook another 5 minutes. Serves 4 to 6.

MENU

Lemony Veal Stew
Warm White Rolls
Cold Chocolate Soufflé

Spanish Chicken Chilindron

In Spain dishes that are cooked in a flavorful sauce of onions, garlic, tomatoes, ham and peppers are called *chilindron*. They are from the region of Aragon.

1 frying chicken, 3-3½ pounds, cut up
salt, pepper to taste
1/3 cup olive or vegetable oil
1 large onion, peeled and sliced
1 garlic clove, minced
3 small red or green peppers, seeded and minced
1/4 pound smoked ham, diced
4 large tomatoes, peeled and chopped
2 canned pimientos, chopped
12 pitted black or green olives

Wash and dry the chicken pieces. Season with salt and pepper. Fry in the heated oil in a skillet until golden on all sides. Remove to a plate. Add the onion, garlic, peppers and ham to the drippings and sauté for 5 minutes. Add the tomatoes and pimientos and cook over medium heat for 5 minutes. Return the chicken pieces to the kettle. Season with salt and pepper. Cover tightly and cook over very low heat about 30 minutes. Add a little water while cooking, if needed. Stir in the olives shortly before serving. Serves 4.

MENU

Spanish Chicken Chilindron
Warm Garlic Bread
Orange Cream Pie

Beer Beef Stew

A good dish for a Saturday night supper.

**2 pounds beef chuck or stew meat,
cut into 1½-inch cubes
3 tablespoons (about) shortening
2 large onions, peeled and sliced
2 tablespoons flour
salt, pepper to taste
2 teaspoons sugar
1/2 teaspoon dried thyme or basil
1 cup (about) beer
1/2 cup beef bouillon or water
4 carrots, scraped and cut up
4 medium-sized potatoes, peeled and cubed**

Dry the beef and brown in the shortening in a Dutch oven. Push aside and add the onions. Sauté until tender. Sprinkle in the flour and season with salt and pepper. Add the sugar, thyme, beer and bouillon and simmer, covered, for 1 hour. Add the carrots and potatoes and continue cooking for about 30 minutes longer, or until the ingredients are cooked. Add a little more beer during the cooking, if needed. Serves 6.

MENU

*Beer Beef Stew
Rye Bread
Warm Apple Pie*

Daube of Duckling

Here is another good French *daube* dish that could be served for a holiday or special occasion dinner.

**1 duckling, 4-5 pounds, cut up
1 cup dry white wine
1/4 cup brandy (optional)
7 tablespoons (about) olive or vegetable oil
1 garlic clove, minced
1 large bay leaf, crumbled**

1/2 teaspoon dried thyme
6 parsley sprigs
salt, pepper to taste
1/2 cup diced smoked ham
1 large onion, peeled and sliced
3 carrots, scraped and sliced thinly
4 medium-sized tomatoes, peeled and chopped
1 cup whole small mushrooms, cleaned
12 pitted black olives

With the duckling pieces and wipe dry. Place in a large shallow dish or crock. Add the wine, brandy, 1/4 cup oil, garlic, bay leaf, thyme, parsley, salt and pepper. Marinate 3-4 hours. Turn over the duckling a few times. When ready to cook, put the ham, 3 tablespoons oil, the onion and carrots in a large skillet or saucepan and sauté for 5 minutes. With a slotted spoon remove the ham and vegetables to a plate. Take the duckling pieces from the marinade and wipe dry. Reserve the marinade. Fry the duckling on all sides in the drippings, adding more oil if needed. Lower the heat, cover and cook over a medium flame, for about 20 minutes, or until most of the grease from the duckling has been released. Spoon off the grease and discard. Return the ham and sautéed vegetables to the dish. Add the tomatoes and marinade. Cook slowly, covered, about 1 hour, or until the duckling is tender. Add the mushrooms and olives 15 minutes before the cooking is finished. Serves 4.

MENU

Daube of Duckling
Crusty White Bread
Fruit Tarts

Irish Stew

This is the traditional preparation for a stew that has become very popular in American restaurants.

**3 pounds breast of lamb
5 medium-sized onions, peeled and sliced
3 pounds (9 medium sized) potatoes, peeled and sliced
salt, pepper to taste
1 tablespoon chopped fresh parsley**

Remove the fat from the lamb and cut into several pieces. In a large saucepan or Dutch oven arrange a layer of the lamb, then a layer of onions and potatoes. Sprinkle each with salt and pepper. Top with the parsley. Add enough water to cover the ingredients. Bring to a boil and remove any scum. Lower the heat, cover and simmer for 2-2½ hours or until the ingredients are well cooked. Add a little more water during the cooking, if needed. Serves 4 to 6.

MENU

*Irish Stew
Soda Bread or Buttermilk Biscuits
Fruit Cake*

Rumanian Chicken Tocana

This well-flavored dish is typical of the *tocanas*, or stews, prepared in Rumania.

**2 frying chickens, about 2½ pounds each, cut up
salt, pepper to taste
2 medium-sized onions, peeled and sliced thinly
2 garlic cloves, crushed
1/3 cup (about) olive or vegetable oil
2 cups dry white wine or chicken broth
1 cup sliced pitted black olives
1/2 cup chopped fresh parsley
1/2 cup sour cream at room temperature**

Wash the chicken pieces and wipe dry. Season with salt and pepper. Sauté the onions and garlic in the oil in a large skillet. Add the chicken pieces and brown on all sides. Add the wine and mix well. Cover and cook slowly for 1 hour. Add the olives, parsley and sour cream. Cook another 5 minutes or until the chicken is tender. Serves 6.

MENU

Rumanian Chicken Tocana
Warm Corn Bread
Fruit Compote
Nut Cookies

Meatball-Fruit Stew

This recipe is inspired by the South American fondness for combining beef and fruit in flavorful stews.

2 pounds lean ground beef
1 cup fine dry breadcrumbs
2 eggs
1 teaspoon dried oregano
salt, pepper to taste
3 tablespoons (about) vegetable oil
2 cups drained pineapple cubes
1 medium-sized green pepper, cleaned and chopped
2 cups chopped canned peaches

In a large bowl combine the beef, breadcrumbs, eggs, oregano, salt and pepper. Mix well and shape into 1½-inch balls. In a kettle or saucepan heat the oil and brown the meatballs on all sides in it, adding more oil if needed. Add 1½ cups of water, cover and cook slowly for 30 minutes. Check a few times to see if more water is needed to keep the meatballs from sticking to the pan. Stir in the remaining ingredients and leave on the stove long enough to heat through. Serves 6 to 8.

MENU

Meatball-Fruit Stew
Warm Whole-Wheat Rolls
Coconut Cream Pudding

Turkish Lamb Pilaf

This is one of the many excellent lamb-rice dishes that have been prepared for centuries in Turkish kitchens.

2 medium-sized onions, peeled and chopped
1/4 cup butter or margarine
2 pounds leg or shoulder of lamb, cut into 1-inch cubes
1/4 cup tomato paste
1 cup tomato juice
1/2 teaspoon dried thyme or oregano
salt, pepper to taste
1½ cups uncooked long grain rice
2 cups (about) chicken broth
1/4 cup chopped fresh parsley

In a kettle or large saucepan sauté the onions in the butter until tender. Push aside and add the lamb cubes, several at a time, to brown on all sides. Mix in the tomato paste, tomato juice, thyme, salt and pepper. Cook slowly, covered, for 1 hour. Add a little water during the cooking, if needed. Mix in the rice and chicken broth and continue to cook slowly for about 30 minutes longer, or until the rice is tender and most of the liquid has been absorbed. It may be necessary to add a little more broth during the cooking if the stew becomes too dry. Do not stir during the cooking. Mix in the parsley just before serving. Serves 4 to 6.

MENU

Turkish Lamb Pilaf
Sesame Seed Bread

Fresh Melon
Chocolate Cookies

Flounder-Sauerkraut Smetana Stew

A good fish-sauerkraut dish flavored with herbs and sour cream.

1 large onion, peeled and chopped
1/3 cup minced carrots
3 tablespoons vegetable oil
1 can (1 pound) sauerkraut, drained
1 can (1 pound) tomatoes, undrained
1 small bay leaf
1/4 teaspoon dried thyme or basil
salt, pepper to taste
1 pound fresh or frozen flounder fillets, cut up
1/8 teaspoon dill seed
1 cup sour cream at room temperature
2 tablespoons minced fresh parsley

Sauté the onion and carrots in the oil in a large skillet or Dutch oven until tender. Add the sauerkraut, and sauté, mixing with a fork, for 2-3 minutes. Add the tomatoes, bay leaf, thyme, salt and pepper and cook slowly, covered, for 20 minutes. Add the flounder and dill seed and water to cover. Cover and cook slowly until the fish is just tender, about 10 minutes. Mix in the sour cream and leave on the stove long enough to heat through. Serve garnished with the parsley. Serves 4.

MENU

Flounder-Sauerkraut Smetana Stew
Warm Parkerhouse Rolls
Cherry Pie à la mode

Spanish Beef-Eggplant Stew

An excellent autumn supper dish.

1 large onion, peeled and chopped
1-2 garlic cloves, crushed
1/4 cup olive or vegetable oil
3 medium-sized tomatoes, peeled and chopped
1 teaspoon paprika
1/2 teaspoon dried oregano
salt, pepper to taste
2 pounds chuck or stew beef, cut into 1½-inch cubes
1 cup (about) beef bouillon or water
1 medium-sized eggplant, washed, stemmed and cut
into small cubes
1/3 cup chopped fresh parsley

In a kettle sauté the onion and garlic in the oil until tender. Mix in the tomatoes, paprika, oregano, salt and pepper. Cook slowly, uncovered, for 5 minutes. Push aside and add the beef cubes, several at a time, and brown in the oil drippings. Add the bouillon or water and bring to a boil. Lower the heat and cook slowly, covered, for 1 hour. Add the eggplant cubes and continue to cook slowly for about 30 minutes longer, or until the ingredients are tender. Mix in the parsley just before serving. Serves 4 to 6.

MENU

Spanish Beef-Eggplant Stew
Crusty White Bread
Fresh Orange Slices with Grated Coconut

Pork and Rice Stew, Chinese-Style

1 cup minced green onions, with tops
2 garlic cloves, crushed
6 tablespoons (about) peanut oil
4 pounds lean boneless pork, cut into 1-inch cubes
2½ cups uncooked long grain rice
5 cups (about) beef bouillon or water
1/3 cup (about) soy sauce
4 slices fresh ginger (optional)
2 teaspoons sugar
pepper to taste
1 can (1 pound) bean sprouts, drained
1 can (8 ounces) bamboo shoots, sliced and drained
1 can (8 ounces) water chestnuts, drained and sliced
3 cups sliced fresh or canned mushrooms
2 medium-sized green peppers, cleaned and sliced

Sauté the onions and garlic in the oil in a kettle until tender. Dry the pork cubes. Push aside the onions and add the pork cubes, several at a time, to brown on all sides. Add more oil, if needed. Add a little water and cook slowly, covered, for 30 minutes. Add the rice, bouillon, soy sauce, ginger, sugar and pepper and mix well. Cover and cook slowly for about 30 minutes or until the ingredients are tender and the liquid is absorbed. Mix in the remaining ingredients and cook another 10 minutes. (The cook may wish to add more soy sauce when adding the last six ingredients. The strength of soy sauce varies considerably, so it is difficult to stipulate the necessary amount for any recipe.) Serves 10 to 12.

MENU

Pork and Rice Stew, Chinese-Style
Assorted Crackers
Fresh Fruit Medley
Almond Cookies

Mulligan Stew

This stew, originally prepared by hobos, was made of any available meats and vegetables, and for some unknown reason came to be known by the Irish name of Mulligan. Over the years the so-called recipes for it have included any number of diverse ingredients, and seemingly every cook has a different version. This is one of the many.

2½ pounds beef chuck or stew beef, cut into 1½-inch cubes
4 tablespoons flour
salt, pepper to taste
3-4 tablespoons shortening
8 cups water
4 large carrots, scraped and sliced thickly
6 medium-sized potatoes, peeled and halved
1 medium-sized head cauliflower, cleaned and cut up
4 large onions, peeled and halved
2 cups green peas
2 cups whole kernel corn
1/2 teaspoon dried thyme
1/2 teaspoon dried marjoram
1/4 cup chopped fresh parsley

Dry the beef cubes and dredge with flour seasoned with salt and pepper. Heat the shortening in a kettle or Dutch oven and brown the meat in it on all sides. Add the water and bring to a boil. Lower the heat, cover and simmer for 1½ hours or until the meat is almost tender. Add the carrots, potatoes, cauliflower and onions and cook 30 minutes. Then add the remaining ingredients and cook about 12 minutes, or until the vegetables are cooked. Serves 8.

MENU

Mulligan Stew
Crusty White Bread
Butterscotch Sundaes

Sweet-Sour Pork-Red Cabbage Stew

A good winter dish, typical of the cooking of Germany and Austria.

1 large onion, peeled and chopped
3 tablespoons lard or shortening
2 pounds lean boneless pork, cut into 1½-inch cubes
1 bay leaf
3 whole cloves
salt, pepper to taste
1 medium-sized head red cabbage, cleaned and finely shredded
2 tart apples, peeled and cubed
1/2 cup wine vinegar
3 tablespoons sugar
3 tablespoons currant jelly (optional)

Fry the onion in the lard in a skillet or Dutch oven until tender. Add the pork and brown on all sides. Add the bay leaf, cloves, salt and pepper, and water to cover. Cover and cook slowly for 1 hour. Add the cabbage and apple and more water, if needed. Continue to cook slowly for about 30 minutes longer, or until the cabbage is tender. Add the vinegar, sugar and jelly during the last 10 minutes of cooking. Serves 6.

MENU

Sweet-Sour Pork-Red Cabbage Stew
Rye Bread
Apple Kuchen

African Chicken-Peanut Butter Stew

The peanut, called a groundnut in Africa, is an essential ingredient in the basic cookery of many countries. Peanut sauces are particularly important to the many West African stews, especially those made with chicken. Generally this dish is flavored with a number of pungent seasonings in addition to the peanut sauce. The following stew is an adaptation that is prepared with peanut butter as a substitute for the homemade ground mixture.

1 frying chicken, about 3½ pounds, cut up
1 large onion, peeled and sliced
2 garlic cloves, crushed
4 tablespoons peanut or vegetable oil
3 large tomatoes, peeled and chopped
1/4 cup tomato paste
2 red or green chilies, washed and seeded, or
1 tablespoon canned chopped green chilies
salt, pepper to taste
1/2 cup (about) peanut butter

Wash the chicken pieces and dry. Sauté the onion and garlic in the oil in a large skillet until tender. Push aside and add the tomatoes, tomato paste, chilies, salt and pepper. Leave uncovered and cook slowly for 5 minutes. Add the chicken pieces and cook in some of the drippings, pushing the sauce aside, until brown. Cover with water, cover and cook slowly for 25 minutes. Mix the peanut butter with some of the hot sauce and stir well. Mix into the chicken and leave on the stove several minutes longer. Check the sauce to determine whether you would like to add more peanut butter. Serves 4.

MENU

African Chicken-Peanut Butter Stew
Warm Corn Muffins
Banana Cream Pie

Easy Veal-Vegetable Stew

A delicious easy-to-prepare stew for a family meal.

1½ pounds stewing veal, cut into 1½-inch cubes
2 tablespoons flour
salt, pepper to taste
1/4 cup vegetable oil or shortening
1 can (1 pound) tomatoes, undrained
1/4 teaspoon dried marjoram or thyme
1 package (9 ounces) frozen cut green beans
1 package (10 ounces) frozen cut corn
1 can (1 pound) small white onions, drained
3 tablespoons chopped fresh parsley

Dry the veal cubes and dust with flour seasoned with salt and pepper. Heat the oil in a skillet or large saucepan and brown the veal in it on all sides. Add the tomatoes, marjoram and water to cover. Cover and simmer for 1½ hours, adding more water during the cooking, if needed. Add the vegetables during the last 10 or 15 minutes of cooking. Mix in the parsley before removing from the stove. Serves 4.

MENU

Easy Veal-Vegetable Stew
Warm Whole-Wheat Rolls
Ice Cream Cake

Short Ribs Jardinière

This is an inviting way to prepare inexpensive short ribs.

4-4½ pounds beef short ribs, cut into 3-inch pieces
flour
salt, pepper to taste
1/4 cup (about) shortening or vegetable oil
2 large onions, peeled and sliced
2 garlic cloves, crushed
1 can (6 ounces) tomato paste
2 cups hot water
2 bay leaves

1/4 teaspoon dried rosemary
2 carrots, scraped and sliced
1 package (9 ounces) frozen cut green beans

Dry the short ribs and dredge with flour that has been seasoned with salt and pepper. Set aside on a plate. Heat the shortening in a skillet and sauté the onions and garlic in it until tender. Push aside and add the short ribs to brown on all sides. Mix in the tomato paste and add the hot water. Mix well. Add the bay leaves and rosemary. Cover and cook slowly for 1½ hours. Add the carrots and cook another 30 minutes, adding the green beans during the last 10 minutes of cooking. Serves 4.

MENU

Short Ribs Jardinière
Crusty White Bread
Lemon Chiffon Cake

Southern Chicken with Dumplings

A simple but good dish for an impromptu meal.

2 pounds chicken thighs
2 cups water
1/2 teaspoon dried parsley
salt, pepper to taste
2 cups frozen mixed vegetables
1 can (1 pound) small white onions, drained
1 cup packaged biscuit mix
1/3 cup milk

Put the chicken, water, parsley, salt and pepper in a large saucepan or kettle. Cover and simmer for 40 minutes or until the chicken is tender. Mix in the vegetables and onions. Combine the biscuit mix and milk and stir lightly. Drop by spoonfuls over the chicken pieces. Cook, uncovered, 10 minutes. Cover and cook 10 minutes longer or until the biscuits are done. Serves 4.

MENU

Southern Chicken with Dumplings
Mixed Green Salad
Chilled Watermelon

Weekend Meatball-Rice Stew

Excellent to serve at a Saturday or Sunday night supper.

1½ pounds ground beef
1 egg, slightly beaten
1 cup fine cracker crumbs
1/4 cup minced onion
2 teaspoons turmeric powder (optional)
salt, pepper to taste
3 tablespoons (about) vegetable oil or shortening
1 can (10½ ounces) condensed tomato soup
1 soup can water
1/4 teaspoon dried thyme or oregano
2 cups frozen baby lima beans
2 cups cooked rice

In a bowl combine the beef, egg, crumbs, onion, turmeric, salt and pepper. Shape into about 24 meatballs. Brown a few at a time in the oil in a large saucepan, or Dutch oven. Mix in the soup, water and thyme. Season with salt and pepper. Cover and cook slowly for 20 minutes. Check now and then to see if a little water is needed to prevent the meatballs from sticking to the pan. Stir in the lima beans and rice and cook about 7 minutes longer, or until the ingredients are cooked. Serves 6.

MENU

Weekend Meatball-Rice Stew
Hot Buttered French Bread
Strawberry Chiffon Pie

Leftover Ham-Lentil Pot

This dish is good and economical.

1 cup dried lentils
1 large onion, peeled and minced
2 garlic cloves, crushed
2 tablespoons vegetable oil
1 can (6 ounces) tomato paste
salt, pepper to taste
1 teaspoon prepared mustard
1 teaspoon Worcestershire sauce
3 cups cubed cooked ham

Wash and pick over the lentils. In a large saucepan or Dutch oven sauté the onion and garlic in the oil until tender. Add the lentils and 3 cups water. Bring to a boil; boil for 2 minutes. Take off the heat and let stand for 1 hour. Return to the stove and mix in the tomato paste, salt and pepper. Cover and cook slowly for 1 hour or until the lentils are tender. Mix in the mustard, Worcestershire and ham and leave on the stove for 5 minutes. Serves 4 to 6.

MENU

Leftover Ham-Lentil Pot
Crusty Dark Bread
Chocolate Nut Cake

Lamb Curry with Peas

This is a type of stew that originated in India many, many years ago. Curry, an important seasoning in Indian cuisine, varies in strength depending on its brand, so you may want to experiment to find the brand and amount that suits your taste.

1 large onion, peeled and minced
2 tablespoons vegetable oil
1-3 tablespoons curry powder
salt, pepper to taste
1/3 cup flour
1 cup chicken broth
2 cups milk
3 cups diced cooked lamb
2 cups green peas

Sauté the onion in the oil in a large saucepan until tender. Add the curry powder, salt and pepper and cook 1 minute. Stir in the flour and then gradually add the broth, stirring as adding, and cook slowly until thickened. Pour in the milk and cook slowly until thickened and smooth. Mix in the lamb and cook slowly for 10 minutes. Then add the peas and cook for 5 minutes. Serves 4.

MENU

Lamb Curry with Peas
Hot Baking Powder Biscuits
Gingered Pineapple Slices

Pork Goulash with Noodles

A different type of goulash, this dish is good for a winter supper or dinner.

2 pounds lean boneless pork, cut into 1½-inch cubes
2 large onions, peeled and sliced
1/4 cup lard or shortening
1-2 tablespoons paprika
1 can (6 ounces) tomato paste
1/2 teaspoon caraway seeds
1 bay leaf
salt, pepper to taste
1 large green pepper, cleaned and chopped
3 cups drained cooked noodles

Dry the pork cubes. Sauté the onions in the lard in a large skillet until tender. Add the paprika and cook 1 minute. Push aside and add the pork cubes, several at a time, and brown in the drippings. Mix in the tomato paste, caraway seeds, bay leaf and water to cover. Season with salt and pepper. Cook slowly, covered, for 1½ hours, adding more water if necessary. Stir in the green pepper and noodles. Leave on the stove long enough to heat through. Remove and discard the bay leaf. Serves 6.

MENU

Pork Goulash with Noodles
Salt Sticks
Fruit-Filled Pancakes

Oxtail Stew Paysanne

Oxtails, a flavorful meat, are often difficult to find, but are well worth looking for as they make interesting dishes such as this one.

2 pounds oxtails, cut into short lengths
flour
salt, pepper to taste
1 large onion, peeled and chopped
1-2 garlic cloves, crushed

1/4 cup diced bacon
2 tablespoons vegetable oil
2 cups (about) beef bouillon or water
1 bay leaf
1/4 teaspoon dried thyme
2 large carrots, scraped and sliced thickly
4 medium-sized potatoes, peeled and halved
4 small turnips, pared and cubed

Dry the oxtail pieces and dredge in flour seasoned with salt and pepper. Set aside on a plate. In a skillet sauté the onion and garlic with the bacon in the oil until tender. Push aside and add the oxtails. Brown on all sides. Add the bouillon, bay leaf and thyme. Bring to a boil. Lower the heat, cover and cook slowly for 3 hours or until tender. Add the carrots, potatoes and turnips during the last 30 minutes of cooking. Serve the oxtails surrounded by the vegetables. Serves 4.

MENU

Oxtail Stew Paysanne
Crusty Dark Bread
Cherry Torte

Pork Hock-Vegetable Stew

Inexpensive pork hocks make an interesting and different stew.

1 large onion, peeled and chopped
3 tablespoons lard or vegetable oil
4 fresh pork hocks
1 bay leaf
1/2 teaspoon celery seed
salt, pepper to taste
4 medium-sized sweet potatoes, peeled
4 medium-sized white turnips, peeled
2 cups frozen cut-up corn

In a kettle sauté the onion in the lard until tender. Push aside and add the hocks. Brown on all sides. Add the bay leaf, celery seed, salt and pepper and water to cover. Bring to a boil. Lower the heat, cover and simmer for 1½ hours. Add the sweet potatoes and turnips and a little more water, if needed. Continue cooking for another 30 minutes or until the ingredients are done. Add the corn during the last 5 minutes of cooking. Serve the hocks on a platter surrounded with the vegetables. Serves 4.

MENU

Pork Hock-Vegetable Stew
Warm Corn Muffins
Pecan Pie

RAGOUTS

Taken from the French word *ragoûter*, meaning "to revive the taste," a ragout denotes a stew that is generally highly seasoned, perhaps with wine, spices or other flavorings.

Prepared with meat, game, poultry or fish, and sometimes with vegetables, ragouts rarely require elaborate ingredients. Some of the best-known brown ragouts are those with mutton or lamb. On the other hand, excellent white ragouts feature such foods as lobster, asparagus tips and truffles. A particular favorite is *civet*, generally made with small game such as hare or rabbit.

Although primarily thought of as a French dish, other cuisines have versions of ragouts. A good ragout can be made with whatever the cook wishes.

Marvelous for sit-down dinners, holidays, or small late-evening get-togethers, a ragout deserves to be served regally with pretty table appointments.

Ragout of Sirloin Tips Jardinière

This elegant ragout is a good dish for a holiday dinner.

3 tablespoons flour
salt and pepper to taste
3 pounds sirloin beef tips, cut into 1½-inch cubes
2 medium-sized onions, peeled and sliced thinly
3-4 tablespoons butter, margarine or vegetable oil
1½ cups (about) dry red wine
1 teaspoon crumbled dried herbs (chives, basil,
thyme or oregano)
1 package (9 ounces) frozen artichoke hearts or
1/2 pound small, fresh artichoke hearts, if available
1 package (10 ounces) frozen cauliflower or
1/2 head fresh cauliflower, broken into small pieces
1 package (10 ounces) frozen zucchini or
1/2 pound fresh zucchini, unpeeled and chopped
2 tablespoons chopped fresh parsley

Put the flour, salt and pepper in a plastic or paper bag and shake the beef cubes in it. Sauté the onions in the heated butter or other fat in a large skillet or saucepan. Push aside and add the floured beef cubes, several at a time, and brown on all sides. Add the wine and herbs; season with salt and pepper. Cover and cook slowly for 30 minutes. Add the frozen vegetables and cook slowly another 15 minutes or longer, until the ingredients are tender. Add more wine during the cooking, if needed. Stir in the parsley. Serves 6 to 8. *Note: If using fresh vegetables, add the cauliflower 30 minutes before the ragout is done; add the remaining vegetables 15 minutes before the end of cooking.*

MENU

Ragout of Sirloin Tips Jardinière
Buttered Boiled Potatoes or Noodles
Warm Croissants
French Pastry

Veal Ragout à la Niçoise

This ragout is prepared in the style of Nice, a resort city in southern France. It includes traditional Niçoise ingredients such as garlic, tomatoes and olives. It is a delectable dish for a sit-down company dinner.

3 pounds boneless shoulder of veal, cut into 1½-inch cubes
3-4 tablespoons olive or vegetable oil
salt, pepper to taste
2 large onions, peeled and sliced
2-3 garlic cloves, crushed
1 cup tomato purée
1½ cups (about) dry white wine
1/4 teaspoon crumbled dried thyme
1/4 teaspoon crumbled dried tarragon
12 flat anchovies, drained and minced
1 cup pitted black olives
3 tablespoons chopped fresh parsley

Dry the veal cubes and brown several at a time in the heated oil in a large skillet. Season with salt and pepper. Remove or push aside and add the onions and garlic. Sauté until tender. Mix the veal cubes with the onions and garlic. Mix in the tomato purée. Add the wine, thyme and tarragon. Bring to a boil. Reduce the heat, cover and cook slowly for about 1½ hours or until the meat is tender. Add more wine during the cooking if needed. Stir in the anchovies, olives and parsley and cook another 5 minutes. Serves 6.

MENU

Veal Ragout à la Niçoise
Buttered Rice
Romaine Lettuce Salad
French Bread
Fresh Strawberry Tarts

Ragout Of Lamb Bonne Femme

Traditional names of foods sometimes have unusual meanings. *Bonne femme*, for example, means "a good wife" in French. In cookery, however, it refers to a preparation of ingredients with mushrooms and white wine. This ragout, which also includes potatoes and tomatoes, is a good spring or summer dinner dish.

2 pounds lamb shoulder, cut into 1½-inch cubes
3-4 tablespoons vegetable oil
1 large onion, peeled and quartered
1 teaspoon sugar
3 tablespoons flour
salt, pepper to taste
1 garlic clove, crushed
1¼ cups (about) dry white wine
1/4 cup tomato purée
2 medium-sized tomatoes, peeled and chopped
bouquet garni **(1 bay leaf, 1/2 teaspoon dried thyme,**
2 parsley sprigs)
6 medium-sized potatoes, peeled and halved
18 medium-sized whole mushrooms, cleaned
3 tablespoons butter or margarine
juice of 1 large lemon

Trim any excess fat from the lamb. Dry and brown several cubes at a time in the heated oil in a large saucepan or Dutch oven. Push aside and add the onion. Sauté until tender. Add the sugar and then the flour; mix well. Season with salt and pepper. Stir in the garlic, wine, tomato purée, tomatoes and *bouquet garni*. Bring to a boil. Lower the heat, cover and cook slowly for 1 hour. Add more wine during the cooking, if needed. Add the potatoes and continue to cook slowly for about 40 minutes longer, until the ingredients are tender. While the lamb mixture is cooking, sauté the mushrooms in the butter and lemon juice in a skillet for 3 minutes. Mix into the ragout 5 minutes before the cooking is finished. Remove and discard the bay leaf and parsley sprigs. Serves 6.

MENU

Ragout Of Lamb Bonne Femme
Mixed Green Salad
Warm Garlic Bread
Ice Cream Bombe

Continental Shrimp-and-Mushroom Ragout

Sour cream imparts a pleasing flavor to this medley of rich ingredients. A good dish for a weekend luncheon.

3 tablespoons minced green onions, with tops
3 tablespoons minced green pepper
3 tablespoons butter, margarine or vegetable oil
2 tablespoons fresh lemon juice
1/2 pound fresh mushrooms, cleaned and sliced
3 tablespoons flour
2 cups light cream or milk
1 pound cooked cleaned shrimp
1½ cups frozen green peas
1/4 teaspoon crumbled dried rosemary
salt, pepper to taste
1 cup sour cream at room temperature
1 tablespoon chopped fresh dill or parsley

Sauté the onions and peppers in the butter in a large sauce-pan or Dutch oven until tender. Add the lemon juice and mushrooms and sauté 4 minutes. Stir in the flour. Gradually add the cream or milk and cook slowly, stirring, until slightly thickened. Mix in the shrimp, peas and rosemary. Season with salt and pepper. Cover and cook slowly for 10 minutes or until the shrimp and peas are tender. Mix in the sour cream and dill and heat through. Serves 4.

MENU

Continental Shrimp-and-Mushroom Ragout
Buttered Rice

Escarole-Radish Salad
Warm Cloverleaf Rolls
Orange Chiffon Pie

Ragout de Boeuf Bourgeoise

Superb hearty dishes prepared *à la bourgeoise* generally include carrots and small onions as well as pieces of braised meat. They are particularly good cold-weather fare.

3 tablespoons flour
salt, pepper to taste
2½ pounds boneless beef chuck or round, cut into
1½-inch cubes
4 thin slices bacon, chopped
2 tablespoons vegetable oil
1½ cups dry vermouth or white wine
3 tablespoons brandy
1/2 cup beef bouillon
1/8 teaspoon dried thyme
1/8 teaspoon dried marjoram
1 garlic clove, crushed
1 small strip orange peel
4 carrots, scraped and sliced thinly
14 small white onions, peeled
2 cups frozen cut-up green beans

Put the flour, salt and pepper in a paper or plastic bag. Wipe the beef cubes to dry them and shake in the flour. Cook the bacon in a large skillet and add the oil. Add the beef cubes, a few at a time, and brown on all sides. Add the vermouth or wine, brandy, bouillon, thyme, marjoram, garlic and orange peel. Season with salt and pepper. Cover and cook slowly for 1 hour. Add the carrots and onions and continue to cook slowly for about 45 minutes longer, or until the ingredients are tender. Add the green beans about 12 minutes before the cooking is finished. Serves 8.

MENU

Ragout de Boeuf Bourgeoise
Sliced Tomato-Cucumber Salad
Crusty Dark Bread
Cherry Soufflé

Rabbit Ragout Chasseur

There are many superb dishes that can be prepared with the tender, mild-flavored meat of the rabbit. This one, enriched with shallots, tomatoes, white wine and mushrooms, is a good summer supper dish.

2 fryer rabbits, about 3 pounds each, cut up
1/3 cup (about) olive or vegetable oil
3 large fresh tomatoes, peeled and chopped, or
3 canned whole tomatoes, chopped
1½ cups (about) dry white wine
1 bay leaf, crumbled
1/2 teaspoon crumbled dried marjoram
salt, pepper to taste
1/4 cup chopped shallots or green onions
3 tablespoons butter or margarine
1 pound small whole or quartered large mushrooms,
cleaned
2 tablespoons minced fresh tarragon, basil or parsley

Dry the rabbit pieces. Heat the oil in a large saucepan or Dutch oven and brown the rabbit pieces, a few at a time in it until golden on all sides. Add the tomatoes, wine, bay leaf, marjoram, salt and pepper. Mix well. Cover and cook slowly 1 hour or longer or until the rabbit is tender. Add more wine during the cooking, if needed. While the rabbit is cooking, sauté the shallots or green onions in the butter in a skillet. Add the mushrooms and sauté for 3 minutes. Mix the onions, mushrooms and the tarragon into the ragout 5 minutes before the cooking is finished. Serves 6.

MENU

Rabbit Ragout Chasseur
Buttered Brown Rice
Bibb Lettuce Salad
Warm Garlic Bread
Ice Cream-Filled Cream Puffs

Balkan Veal and Pork Ragout

This is a typical ragout of the Balkan countries where flavorful meat and vegetable dishes are served at convivial family and holiday celebrations.

1½ pounds boneless veal shoulder,
cut into 1½-inch cubes
1½ pounds lean boneless pork,
cut into 1½-inch cubes
flour
salt, pepper to taste
3 tablespoons (about) vegetable oil
2 garlic cloves, crushed
2 large onions, peeled and sliced
1 cup (about) hot bouillon or water
1/2 cup dry white wine
1/2 teaspoon crumbled dried thyme or oregano
3 large carrots, scraped and cut into 1½-inch pieces
8 small or 4 medium potatoes, peeled and cut into halves
1 package (10 ounces) frozen zucchini or
1/2 pound fresh zucchini
1 tablespoon chopped fresh dill or parsley

Dry the meat cubes and sprinkle with flour, salt and pepper. In a large pan brown a few meat cubes at a time in the oil. Push aside and add the garlic and onions. Sauté until tender. Add the bouillon, wine, thyme, salt and pepper. Bring to a boil. Lower the heat, cover and cook slowly for 1½ hours. Add the carrots after cooking 1 hour. After cooking 1½ hours, add the potatoes and continue cooking another 30 minutes longer, or until the ingredients are tender. Mix in the zucchini 20 minutes before the end of the cooking. Stir in the dill when the ragout is finished cooking. Serves 8.

MENU

Balkan Veal and Pork Ragout
Romaine Lettuce Salad
Crusty Dark Bread
Honey or Spice Cake

Ragout de Veau Marengo

An excellent veal ragout that could be served for a late evening supper.

3 pounds shoulder veal, cut into 1½-inch cubes
3-4 tablespoons olive or vegetable oil
1 large onion, peeled and chopped
2 tablespoons flour
1 cup dry white wine
3/4 cup beef bouillon
1/2 cup tomato purée
2 garlic cloves, halved
***bouquet garni* (1 bay leaf, 1/2 teaspoon dried thyme,**
2 parsley sprigs)
1 small strip orange peel
salt, pepper to taste
1/2 pound fresh mushrooms, cleaned
3 tablespoons chopped fresh parsley

Dry the veal cubes and brown, a few pieces at a time, in the heated oil in a skillet. Push aside and add the onion. Sauté until tender. Stir in the flour. Pour in the wine and bouillon and bring to a boil. Boil for 1 minute. Stir in the tomato purée, garlic, *bouquet garni*, orange peel, salt and pepper. Lower the heat, cover and cook slowly for 1¼ hours or until the meat is tender. Add the mushrooms during the last 10 minutes of cooking. Stir in the parsley just before serving. Remove and discard the bay leaf and parsley sprigs. Serves 6.

MENU

Ragout de Veau Marengo
Parsley Boiled Potatoes
Hearts of Lettuce Salad
Warm Garlic Bread
Peach Short Cake

Ragout of Chicken Orientale

This is an especially good summer luncheon dish.

8 large chicken breasts, split in half
6 tablespoons (about) peanut or vegetable oil
salt, pepper to taste
2/3 cup pineapple juice
4-6 tablespoons soy sauce
1 cup chicken broth or bouillon
1 cup wine vinegar
2/3 cup sliced water chestnuts
2/3 cup sugar
6 tablespoons minced fresh ginger
3 cups drained crushed pineapple
6 tablespoons cornstarch
1/2 cup water
2 large green peppers, cleaned and chopped

Remove the skin from each chicken breast. Sauté the chicken breasts on both sides in the oil in a large kettle or skillet. Season with salt and pepper. Add the pineapple juice, cover and cook slowly for 15 minutes. Remove from the stove and cool. With a knife take off all the meat from the breasts. Discard the bones. Cut the meat into bite-sized pieces and return to the cooking dish. Add the soy sauce, chicken broth, vinegar, water chestnuts, sugar, ginger and pineapple. Cook slowly, covered, for 30 minutes, long enough to blend the flavors. Dissolve the cornstarch in the water and stir into the chicken mixture. Cook slowly, stirring frequently, for several minutes, until thickened. Add the green peppers just before removing from the heat. Serves 8.

MENU

Ragout of Chicken Orientale
Buttered Rice or Fine Noodles
Snow Peas Vinaigrette
Crisp Crackers
Fresh Fruit
Almond Cookies

Basque Ragout of Lamb and Vegetables

The Basque region of northwest Spain and southwest France is famous for its good cooking. Fine ingredients typical of the area are used in this appealing ragout. A good dish for a Sunday supper.

2 pounds lamb shoulder, cut into 1½-inch cubes
3 tablespoons olive or vegetable oil
1 large onion, peeled and sliced
1 garlic clove, crushed
1 medium-sized eggplant, about 1¼ pounds,
unpeeled and cut into small cubes
1 can (6 ounces) tomato paste
1½ cups (about) hot water
1/4 teaspoon each of crumbled dried thyme and marjoram
salt, pepper to taste
6 medium-sized potatoes, peeled and halved
1 jar (4 ounces) pimientos, chopped
2 tablespoons chopped fresh parsley

Remove any excess fat from the lamb. Dry and brown a few pieces at a time in the oil in a kettle. Push aside and add the onion and garlic. Sauté until tender. Add the eggplant, tomato paste, water, thyme, marjoram, salt and pepper and mix well. Cover and cook slowly 1 hour. Add the potatoes and cook about 30 minutes longer or until tender. Pour in a little more water during the cooking, if needed. Add the pimientos and parsley 5 minutes before the cooking is finished. Serves 6.

MENU

Basque Ragout of Lamb and Vegetables
Mixed Green Salad
Warm Garlic Bread
Orange Bavarian Cream

Ragout de Boeuf Bordelaise

This flavorful stew, made with a good dry red wine from the region of Bordeaux, is one of the best French ragouts.

**3 pounds beef sirloin, round or chuck,
cut into 2-inch cubes
flour
salt, pepper to taste
1/4 cup olive or vegetable oil
3/4 cup minced green onions, with tops
1 large garlic clove, crushed
2 cups (about) red Bordeaux wine
2 parsley sprigs
1 small bay leaf
1/2 teaspoon dried thyme
1/2 pound fresh mushrooms, cleaned and sliced
lengthwise into halves
1 can (1 pound) small white onions, drained**

Dry the beef cubes and dredge with flour, seasoned with salt and pepper. Brown on all sides in the heated oil in a large kettle. Push aside and add the green onions and garlic. Sauté until tender. Add the wine, parsley, bay leaf and thyme. Season with salt and pepper. Bring to a boil. Lower the heat, cover and cook slowly about 1½ hours or until the meat is tender. Add the mushrooms and onions 10 minutes before the cooking is finished. Remove and discard the parsley sprigs and bay leaf. Serves 6.

MENU

Ragout de Boeuf Bordelaise
Buttered Green Noodles
Endive Salad
French Bread
Babas au Rhum

Duckling Civet

Although the French word *civet* is used generally for ragouts made with small game and flavored with red wine, mushrooms and onions, the word is derived from *cive*, which means green onions. Probably they were an important ingredient when the dish was created. Duckling is a good substitute for the game. This is an elegant company dinner.

4 thin slices bacon, chopped
2-3 tablespoons vegetable oil
6 shallots or green onions, with tops, minced
1-2 garlic cloves, crushed
2 ducklings, 4-5 pounds each, cut into serving pieces
3 tablespoons flour
1½ cups (about) dry red wine
1 cup beef bouillon
1/4 cup tomato purée
1/3 cup brandy
1 bay leaf
3 parsley sprigs
1/4 teaspoon dried thyme
1/4 teaspoon dried rosemary

salt, pepper to taste
24 small white onions, peeled
24 whole mushrooms, cleaned

Cook the bacon in a large kettle for 1 or 2 minutes. Add the oil, shallots or onions, and garlic; sauté until tender. Add the duckling pieces, a few at a time, and brown on all sides. Mix in the flour to blend well. Add the wine, bouillon, purée, brandy, bay leaf, parsley, thyme, rosemary, salt and pepper. Mix and bring to a boil. Lower the heat, cover and cook slowly for 1 hour. Add the onions and continue to cook slowly about 30 minutes longer, or until the ducklings and onions are tender. Add the mushrooms during the last 10 minutes of cooking. Remove and discard the bay leaf and parsley. Serves 6 to 8.

MENU

Duckling Civet
Parsley Potatoes
Bibb Lettuce Salad
French Bread
Camembert Cheese

Curried Lamb Ragout Indienne

Yogurt is a main ingredient of this ragout.

1 large onion, peeled and chopped
1 garlic clove, crushed
1/4 cup peanut or vegetable oil
1 teaspoon ground turmeric
1 teaspoon ground coriander (optional)
1-2 tablespoons curry powder
salt, pepper to taste
2 pounds boneless lamb, trimmed of fat,
cut into 1½-inch cubes

1/2 cup (about) tomato juice
1 cup plain yogurt at room temperature

Sauté the onion and garlic in the oil in a large saucepan or Dutch oven. Stir in the turmeric, coriander, curry powder, salt and pepper. Cook 1 minute. Dry the lamb cubes and brown, several at a time, on all sides. Add the tomato juice and bring to a boil. Lower the heat and cook slowly, covered, for 1 hour. Stir in the yogurt and continue to cook slowly for another 30 minutes, or until the ingredients are cooked. Add more tomato juice during the first hour of cooking, if needed. Serves 6.

MENU

Curried Lamb Ragout Indienne
Boiled Rice
Mixed Green Salad
Crisp Crackers
Lemon Sherbet with Chocolate Sauce

Chinese Pork-Vegetable Ragout

A flavorful Oriental ragout that is good for a Sunday night supper.

6 green onions, with tops, chopped
2 garlic cloves, crushed
3 thin slices gingerroot (optional)
1/4 cup peanut or vegetable oil
2 pounds lean boneless pork, cut into 1½-inch cubes
1 cup soy sauce
2 tablespoons dry sherry
2 tablespoons sugar
pepper to taste
2 cups shredded Chinese cabbage
2 cups shredded spinach

1 cup sliced mushrooms
1 package (6 ounces) snow peas
1/2 cup sliced bamboo shoots

Sauté the onions, garlic and gingerroot in the oil in a large wok or skillet until tender. Add the pork, several cubes at a time, and brown on all sides. Add the soy sauce, sherry, sugar and pepper. Cover and cook slowly for 1 hour. Add a little water during the cooking, if needed. Mix in the cabbage, spinach, mushrooms, snow peas and bamboo shoots. Continue cooking for about 15 minutes, or until the ingredients are tender. The vegetables should not cook too long. Serves 6.

MENU

Chinese Pork-Vegetable Ragout
Steamed Rice
Orange Sherbet with Chopped Pineapple

Lamb-Eggplant Ragout Italiana

This ragout, made with favorite Italian foods, is good for a weekend luncheon.

3 pounds boneless shoulder or leg of lamb, cut into
1½-inch cubes
3 medium-sized onions, peeled and chopped
2 garlic cloves, crushed
6 tablespoons (about) olive or vegetable oil
1 can (6 ounces) tomato paste
2 cups (about) dry red wine
1 bay leaf
1/2 teaspoon dried thyme
salt, pepper to taste
1 large eggplant, stemmed and cubed
3 tablespoons chopped fresh parsley

Dry the lamb cubes and set aside. In a large saucepan sauté the onions and garlic in the oil until tender. Push aside and add the lamb, several cubes at a time, and brown on all sides. Mix in the tomato paste. Add the wine, bay leaf, thyme, salt and pepper. Cook slowly, covered, for 1 hour, adding more wine, if needed. Add the eggplant and continue cooking for about 30 minutes longer, or until the ingredients are cooked. Remove and discard the bay leaf. Mix in the parsley. Serves 6 to 8.

MENU

Lamb-Eggplant Ragout Italiana
Warm Garlic Bread
Canned Pears with Whipped Cream

Viennese Oxtail Ragout

This is another excellent oxtail dish, good for a winter dinner.

2 pounds oxtails, cut into short lengths
flour
salt, pepper to taste
2 medium-sized onions, peeled and chopped
2 carrots, scraped and diced
1/4 cup shortening
2 tablespoons paprika
2 cups (about) beef bouillon
1/4 teaspoon dried oregano
2 cups frozen green peas
1 cup sour cream at room temperature
1 tablespoon chopped fresh dill or parsley

Dry the oxtail pieces and dredge in flour seasoned with salt and pepper. Set aside on a plate. In a saucepan sauté the onions and carrots in the shortening until tender. Mix in the paprika and cook for 1 minute. Push aside and add the oxtails. Brown on all sides. Add the bouillon and oregano and bring to a boil. Lower the heat, cover and cook slowly for 2½-3 hours until tender. Add more bouillon during the cooking, if needed. Mix in the peas, sour cream and dill and heat through. Serves 4.

MENU

Viennese Oxtail Ragout
Warm Boiled Potatoes
Poppy-Seed Rolls
Chocolate Torte

Shrimp and Artichoke Ragout

An elegant ragout that would be good for a light luncheon.

1/2 cup minced green onions, with tops
1/3 cup minced green pepper
1/4 cup minced celery
3 tablespoons butter or margarine
1 can (1 pound) tomatoes, undrained
1 can (8 ounces) tomato sauce
1 cup (about) dry white wine
1 medium bay leaf
1/2 teaspoon dried thyme
2 parsley sprigs
dash cayenne
salt, pepper to taste
1½ pounds raw shrimp, shelled and deveined
2 packages (9 ounces each) frozen artichoke hearts

In a saucepan or skillet sauté the onions, green pepper and celery in the butter until tender. Mix in the tomatoes, tomato sauce, wine, bay leaf, thyme, parsley, cayenne, salt and pepper. Cook slowly, uncovered, for 10 minutes. Add the shrimp, cover and continue cooking for 30 minutes. Add the artichoke hearts and cook about 10 minutes longer or until the ingredients are tender. Remove the bay leaf and parsley before serving. Serves 6.

MENU

Shrimp and Artichoke Ragout
Buttered Cooked Rice
Warm Whole-Wheat Rolls
Lemon Meringue Pie

Boeuf en Piperade Ragout

Another ragout from southern France, this is good for an informal company buffet.

3 pounds boneless beef chuck or stew beef, cut into
2-inch cubes
flour
salt, pepper to taste
2 large onions, peeled and sliced
2 garlic cloves, crushed
5 tablespoons (about) olive or vegetable oil
3 large tomatoes, peeled and chopped
1 can (8 ounces) tomato sauce
1 teaspoon dried basil or oregano
***bouquet garni* (1 bay leaf, 1/2 teaspoon dried thyme,**
4 parsley sprigs, wrapped in cheesecloth)
1½ cups (about) dry red wine
2 medium-sized green peppers, cleaned and sliced
2 cans pimientos, cut into strips
1 cup sliced pitted green or black olives

Dry the beef cubes and dredge in flour seasoned with salt and pepper. Set aside. In a large skillet sauté the onions and garlic in the oil until tender. Push aside and add the beef cubes, several at a time, and brown on all sides. Add more oil, if needed. Add the tomatoes, tomato sauce, basil and *bouquet garni*. Pour in the wine, cover and cook slowly for 1½ hours, adding more wine, if needed. Mix in the remaining ingredients and cook another 5 minutes, until the ingredients are tender. Remove the *bouquet garni*. Serves 6 to 8.

MENU

Boeuf en Piperade Ragout
Warm Garlic Bread
Ice Cream-Filled Cream Puffs

Ragout of Pork Stroganoff

This sour cream-flavored pork dish is elegant enough for a company dinner.

2 pounds lean boneless pork
6 tablespoons (about) butter or margarine
1 medium-sized onion, peeled and chopped
1/2 pound fresh mushrooms, cleaned and sliced
3 tablespoons tomato paste
1 tablespoon prepared mustard
1 cup dry white wine
pinch sugar
salt, pepper to taste
2 teaspoons flour
1 cup sour cream at room temperature

Remove any fat from the pork and cut into strips about 1 inch thick and 3 inches long. Heat 2 tablespoons of butter in a large saucepan or skillet. Add some of the pork and brown quickly. Remove to a plate. Finish browning the pork. Sauté the onion in the drippings. Add the mushrooms and more butter, if needed. Sauté 4 minutes. Stir in the tomato paste and mustard. Add the wine, sugar, salt and pepper. Bring to a boil. Lower the heat, cover and cook slowly for 10 minutes. Combine the flour and sour cream and leave on the stove long enough to cook slightly, 5 to 7 minutes. Serves 4.

MENU

Ragout of Pork Stroganoff
Buttered Rice

Mixed Green Salad
Crusty White Bread
French Pastries

Côte d'Azur Chicken-Vegetable Ragout

This highly seasoned ragout originated on France's southern coast. It is a good dish for a late evening supper.

1 frying chicken, about 2½ pounds, cut up
2 medium-sized onions, peeled and sliced
1-2 garlic cloves, crushed
1/4 cup butter or margarine
3 large tomatoes, peeled and chopped
1½ cups (about) dry white wine
1 teaspoon dried tarragon or basil
salt, pepper to taste
2 medium zucchini, sliced
2 medium green peppers, cleaned and sliced
3 tablespoons chopped fresh parsley

Dry the chicken pieces and set aside. In a skillet sauté the onions and garlic in the butter until tender. Push aside and add the chicken. Brown on all sides until golden. Add the tomatoes, wine, tarragon, salt and pepper. Cover and cook slowly for 15 minutes. Add the zucchini and peppers and continue cooking about 20 minutes longer, or until the ingredients are tender. Mix in the parsley before serving. Serves 4.

MENU

Côte d'Azur Chicken-Vegetable Ragout
Crusty White Bread
Strawberry Ice Cream with Chocolate Sauce

Fruited Lamb and Rice Ragout

This is an excellent dish to serve at an outdoor meal.

**2 pounds boneless lamb shoulder or leg,
cut into 2-inch cubes
1/2 cup diced celery
1/2 cup diced onion
1/2 cup diced green pepper
1/4 cup butter or margarine
2 cups (about) orange juice
1 teaspoon grated orange rind
dash nutmeg
salt, pepper to taste
2 cups cooked rice
1 cup diced fresh oranges
1 cup diced fresh or canned peaches
1 cup diced fresh or canned pears
1 tablespoon chopped fresh mint**

Trim any excess fat from the lamb cubes. Wipe dry and set aside. Sauté the celery, onion and green pepper in the butter in a Dutch oven. When tender push aside, and add the lamb cubes, several at a time, and brown on all sides. Add the orange juice, orange rind, nutmeg, salt and pepper. Cover and cook slowly for 1½ hours, adding more juice during the cooking if needed. Mix in the remaining ingredients and more juice, if necessary, and leave on the stove long enough to heat through. Serves 6.

MENU

*Fruited Lamb and Rice Ragout
Crusty White Bread
Chocolate Ice Cream with Grated Coconut*

Parisian Ragout de Sole

An easy-to-prepare ragout that could be served for a light luncheon.

3 tablespoons minced shallots or green onions
3 tablespoons butter or margarine
2 tablespoons fresh lemon juice
1 cup sliced fresh mushrooms
3 tablespoons flour
1 cup dry white wine
2½ cups (about) light cream or milk
dash cayenne
salt, pepper to taste
2 pounds sole or flounder fillets, cut into
serving pieces
1 cup cooked asparagus tips
1 cup cooked cleaned shrimp

Sauté the shallots in the butter in a large saucepan until tender. Add the lemon juice and mushrooms and sauté until tender, about 4 minutes. Mix in the flour and cook 1 minute. Slowly add the wine and then the cream or milk; stir constantly until thickened and smooth. Season with cayenne, salt and pepper. Add the fish pieces, cover and cook slowly for about 7 minutes or until they are just tender. Add a little more cream or milk, if desired. Mix in the asparagus and shrimp, and leave on the stove long enough to heat through. Serves 4 to 6.

MENU

Parisian Ragout de Sole
Buttered Rice
Warm Whole-Wheat Rolls
Ice Ceam Cake

Hawaiian Duckling Ragout

An excellent dish for a small holiday dinner.

1 duckling, 4-5 pounds, cut into serving pieces
1 tablespoon peanut or vegetable oil
1 cup orange juice

1 cup (about) pineapple juice
1 teaspoon minced gingerroot (optional)
2 tablespoons soy sauce
pepper to taste
1 cup pineapple tidbits, drained
1 medium-sized green pepper, cleaned and diced

Wash the duckling and wipe dry. Brown on all sides in hot oil in a Dutch oven for 30 minutes. Remove and pour off all the fat except 3 tablespoons. Add the orange and pineapple juices, gingerroot, soy sauce and pepper. Bring to a boil. Lower the heat, cover and cook slowly for 1½-2 hours or until tender. Add the remaining ingredients during the last 5 minutes of cooking. Serves 4.

MENU

Hawaiian Duckling Ragout
Buttered Noodles
Avocado-Lettuce Salad
Coconut Cream Cake

Swedish Seafood Ragout

A good dish for a late evening supper.

1 large onion, peeled and chopped
1/3 cup butter or margarine
3 tablespoons flour
2 cups fish or clam broth
2 cups (about) dry white wine
3 tablespoons tomato paste
1/2 teaspoon dried marjoram
salt, pepper to taste
1 pound white-fleshed fish fillets (cod, haddock, flounder), cut into serving pieces
2 cups flaked cooked salmon
2 cups cleaned medium shrimp

2 cups sour cream at room temperature
2 tablespoons chopped fresh dill

In a large saucepan or kettle sauté the onion in the butter until tender. Mix in the flour and cook 1 minute. Gradually add the fish or clam broth, stirring as adding, and cook slowly until thickened and smooth. Add the wine, tomato paste, marjoram, salt, pepper and fish. Cover and cook slowly for about 7 minutes, or until the fish is just tender. Add more wine during the cooking, if needed. Mix in the salmon, shrimp and sour cream, and continue to cook over low heat until the ingredients are heated. Serve garnished with the dill. Serves 4.

MENU

Swedish Seafood Ragout
Boiled Small Potatoes
Cucumber Salad
Warm Berry Pie

Tuscan Sausage-Bean Ragout

This ragout comes from the northern Italian region of Tuscany, where white beans and sausages are favorite foods. It is a hearty dish, especially welcome on a winter supper table.

1 cup dried white beans
2 medium-sized onions, peeled and chopped
2 garlic cloves, crushed
3 tablespoons bacon fat or shortening
1 can (1 pound) tomatoes, undrained
1 can (6 ounces) tomato paste
1 teaspoon dried rosemary or thyme
salt, pepper to taste
1 pound pork sausage links, fried, drained and cut up
3 tablespoons chopped fresh parsley

Wash the beans and cover with cold water. Bring to a boil and boil for 2 minutes. Let stand for 1 hour. In a kettle sauté the onions and garlic in the fat until tender. Mix in the tomatoes, tomato paste, rosemary, salt and pepper. Cook slowly, uncovered, for 5 minutes. Add the beans and water. Cover and simmer for 1-1½ hours, until the beans are tender. Add more water during the cooking, if needed. Mix in the sausages 5 minutes before the cooking is finished and leave on the stove long enough to heat through. Serve garnished with the parsley. Serves 4.

MENU

Tuscan Sausage-Bean Ragout
Mixed Green Salad
Crusty White Bread
Gorgonzola Cheese
Crackers

Sherried Oyster and Chicken Ragout

A good ragout for a luncheon or a late evening supper.

2 tablespoons minced chives
2 tablespoons minced shallots or green onions
1/2 cup minced green pepper
4 tablespoons butter or margarine
3 tablespoons flour
4 cups light cream or milk
1/4 teaspoon freshly grated nutmeg
salt, pepper to taste
2 cups diced cooked chicken
1 pint fresh oysters, drained
3 tablespoons dry sherry

In a large saucepan sauté the chives, shallots and green pepper in the butter until tender. Mix in the flour and cook slowly, stirring, for 1 minute. Gradually add the cream or milk, stirring constantly, until thickened and smooth. Season with nutmeg, salt and pepper. Add the chicken and oysters and cook gently about 5 minutes, or until the edges of the oysters curl. Remove from the heat and mix in the sherry. Serve at once. Serves 4.

MENU

Sherried Oyster and Chicken Ragout
Warm White Rolls
Bibb Lettuce Salad
Bombe au Chocolat

Southwestern Ragout de Veau

A hearty highly flavored ragout that is a good outdoor dinner dish.

2½ pounds boneless veal shoulder, cut into 2-inch cubes
flour
salt, pepper to taste
2 large onions, peeled and chopped
2 garlic cloves, crushed
5 tablespoons (about) lard or vegetable oil
1-2 tablespoons chili powder
1 teaspoon crumbled dried oregano
salt, pepper to taste
1 can (1 pound) tomatoes, undrained
1 can (8 ounces) tomato sauce
dash hot pepper sauce
2 cups frozen cut-up corn
1 can (1 pound) red kidney beans
1 can (6 ounces) green chilies, chopped

Dry the veal cubes and dredge in flour seasoned with salt and pepper. In a large saucepan, sauté the onions and garlic in the lard or oil until tender. Mix in the chili powder, oregano, salt and pepper and cook 1 minute. Push aside and add the veal cubes, several at a time, and brown on all sides, adding more oil if needed. Add the tomatoes, tomato sauce, and hot pepper sauce. Cover and cook slowly for about 1½ hours, or until the veal is tender. Add a little water during the cooking, if needed. Add the corn, beans and chilies during the last 5 minutes of cooking. Serves 6.

MENU

Southwestern Ragout de Veau
Warm Corn Muffins
Peach Pie

Ragout of Salmon and Tomatoes

This is a good luncheon ragout.

1 medium-sized onion, peeled and chopped
1 medium-sized green pepper, cleaned and minced
2 tablespoons butter or margarine
3 tablespoons flour
1 cup milk
1 can (1 pound) tomatoes, undrained
1/2 teaspoon crumbled dried oregano or thyme
salt, pepper to taste
1 can (1 pound) salmon, drained and flaked

In a large saucepan sauté the onion and green pepper in the butter until the onion is tender. Mix in the flour and cook 1 minute. Gradually add the milk and the liquid of the tomatoes, stirring constantly. Cook slowly, stirring, until thickened and smooth. Add the tomatoes and break up with a spoon or fork. Add the oregano, salt and pepper and cook slowly, being careful not to boil, for 10 minutes. Mix in the salmon and cook another 5 minutes. Serves 4 to 6.

MENU

Ragout of Salmon and Tomatoes
Buttered Rice
Whole-Wheat Muffins
Cherry Cobbler

Polynesian Meatball-Fruit Ragout

A good ragout for an outdoor meal.

1 pound ground lean beef
1/2 pound ground lean pork
1/2 cup fine dry bread crumbs
2 tablespoons minced green onions
1 garlic clove, crushed
2 teaspoons minced gingerroot (optional)
2 tablespoons soy sauce
salt, pepper to taste
2-3 tablespoons peanut or vegetable oil
1½ cups beef bouillon or 1½ beef bouillon cubes
and 1½ cups water
3 tablespoons cornstarch
1/4 cup cider vinegar
1/4 cup sugar
1 can (13¼ ounces) pineapple tidbits, undrained
2 cans (11 ounces each) mandarin oranges, drained
1 cup canned apricot halves
1 large green pepper, cleaned and cubed

Combine the beef, pork, bread crumbs, onions, garlic, gingerroot, soy sauce, salt and pepper in a large bowl. Mix thoroughly. Shape into tiny balls. The mixture should make about 8 dozen meatballs. Heat 1 tablespoon of the oil in a kettle or skillet and brown the meatballs, several at a time, adding oil as needed. Add the bouillon, cover and cook slowly for 25 minutes. Combine the cornstarch with the vinegar. Then mix in the sugar. Stir into the meatball mixture. Add the juice from the pineapple tidbits and mix well. Stir in the fruits and green pepper, and cook over low heat, stirring once or twice, until the ingredients are heated. Serves 6 to 8.

MENU

Polynesian Meatball-Fruit Ragout
Buttered Egg Noodles
Crisp Crackers
Vanilla Ice Cream with Chocolate Sauce

Lobster and Crabmeat Ragout

An elegant ragout for a late evening supper.

3 tablespoons minced shallots or green onions
1/4 cup minced green peppers
1/4 cup butter or margarine
3 tablespoons flour
1/2 teaspoon grated nutmeg
1/2 teaspoon Worcestershire
dash cayenne
salt, pepper to taste
3-4 cups milk
2 cups diced cooked lobster
2 cups cleaned flaked crabmeat
1 cup heavy cream

Sauté the shallots or onions and green peppers in the butter in a large saucepan or kettle until tender. Mix in the flour to form a *roux* and cook 1 minute. Add the nutmeg, Worcestershire, cayenne, salt and pepper. Gradually add the milk, stirring as adding, and cook slowly, stirring occasionally, until thickened and smooth. Add the lobster and crabmeat and cook long enough to heat the ingredients. Gradually add the cream and cook slowly until heated. Serves 4.
Note: Vary the amount of milk according to the desired thickness of the sauce.

MENU

Lobster and Crabmeat Ragout
Romaine Salad
Warm Cloverleaf Rolls
Jam-Filled Crêpes

GLOSSARY

beurre manié   Kneaded or manipulated butter that is made by working flour and butter into tiny balls that are added to sauces, soups and stews as thickening agents. They must be added at the end of the cooking process, and the liquid should not be permitted to boil after they have been added.

bisque   A rich cream soup generally made with fish or shellfish and sometimes with puréed vegetables.

blanquette   A meat or poultry stew with a lemon-flavored cream sauce. It also contains small white onions and mushrooms.

bouillon   A clarified clear broth made by simmering meat, fish or vegetables with seasonings in liquid and then straining. The process is designed to extract their flavors. It is served alone as a soup or used as a base in making soups, stews and sauces.

bouillon cube	A concentrated, dehydrated form of bouillon that is a convenient substitute for the homemade variety.
bouquet garni	Aromatic herbs, fresh and/or dried, which are tied together or enclosed in a small cheesecloth bag and used during cooking to flavor stocks, soups and stews. It usually includes parsley, thyme and bay leaf, to which spices can be added. The *bouquet garni* is always removed and discarded before the dish is served.
braise	Long, slow process of cooking meats and vegetables that includes browning in a little fat and then simmering, tightly covered, in a small amount of liquid. Braising is generally done on top of the stove, but sometimes is done in the oven.
broth	An unclarified thin liquid in which meat, fish or vegetables have been cooked. It is also a soup.
burgoo	A thick stew made with various kinds of meats and vegetables, traditionally cooked in Kentucky in large iron pots for outdoor get-togethers.
casserole	A deep heavy dish with a tight-fitting lid in which foods can be cooked slowly. Also, a combination of foods that were cooked slowly on top of the stove or in the oven.
chowder	A thick, hearty soup made with fish or seafood, or sometimes vegetables, that are cooked in a seasoned milk liquid.
civet	A ragout generally made with small game, particularly rabbit, red wine, onions, mushrooms and the blood of the animal. This term also applies to a stew of *langouste* or spiny lobster.
clarify	Method of removing impurities such as fat and scum from liquids, as well as foods such as butter. Stocks and soups,

after being degreased, are generally clarified by cooking briefly with egg whites and shells and then straining through cheesecloth.

cocido   A Spanish stew made with chickpeas, vegetables and various meats.

cocotte   A French fireproof, oval or round, heavy cooking dish similar to a casserole.

consommé   A clarified clear soup made by reducing or boiling down either chicken or beef bouillon. It is served alone as a soup or used as a base in making various dishes.

correct   Process of modifying or increasing a flavor by the addition of more salt, pepper or other seasonings.

court bouillon   A flavored liquid in which fish or shellfish are simmered. Very often the liquid includes wine and vegetables. It can be used for poaching fish or in making sauces.

crouton   A small piece of bread, generally in the form of a cube, which is either fried in fat or browned in the oven. Croutons are often served as a garnish, particularly in soups.

daube   Method of cooking meat or poultry slowly in a red wine stock with vegetables and seasonings. Also the name of a stew prepared in this manner.

deglaze   To dissolve the brown particles or pan drippings left in a pan by scraping and heating them with added liquid, generally water.

degrease   To remove the accumulated fat from the surface of stocks, soups or stews by either of two methods. From hot liquids, the fat is skimmed off with a spoon or skimmer; or the liquid can be cooled and put in the refrigerator, uncovered, until the fat hardens and can be scraped off.

dredge	To sprinkle food with flour, sugar or some other dry ingredients.
dutch oven	A large heavy kettle or pot with a tight-fitting lid, often made of cast iron. It is frequently used for making soups and stews.
estofado	A stew popular in Spain and South America.
estouffat	A stew popular in the Languedoc region of France. Its primary ingredients are generally dried beans and pork.
fines herbes	A mixture of chopped fresh and/or dried herbs, such as chives, parsley, tarragon and chervil, that is used to flavor soups, stews and other foods.
flambé	Method of setting a dish afire by pouring flaming brandy or another liquor over it and lighting it before the cooking process or just before serving. The alcohol burns off, leaving a desirable flavor.
fricassee	Method of preparing poultry by stewing slowly, then adding a white sauce. The term once meant any stew made with pieces of poultry, meat, fish or vegetables, and cooked in a brown or white stock.
goulash	A Hungarian stew made with varying ingredients, but generally flavored with paprika and very often with sour cream.
gumbo	A thick well-seasoned Creole soup that takes its name from the Bantu word for *okra*, which is a main ingredient. Other ingredients include filé powder—thickening agent as in okra, tomatoes, green peppers, meat, fish, or shellfish in varying combiantions.
haricot	Small white bean, dried or fresh, often used in soups and stews from France.
hotch-potch	One of several similar names given to thick soups or stews made of various ingredients and which are enjoyed in

several European countries. Among them are the English hot pot, Scotch hotch potch, Dutch *hutspot* and French *hochepot*.

lard   To insert strips of fat *(lardoons)* into lean meat before cooking to make it more juicy. This is done generally with a larding needle.

marinade   A seasoned liquid mixture in which food is soaked in order to tenderize it or to add further flavor.

marmite   A very large metal or earthenware French cooking pot that is used for making stocks and soups.

marrowbone   A large beef bone that holds a fatty filling called marrow. It is excellent for enriching such dishes as stocks, soups and stews.

matelote   A fish stew flavored with red or white wine.

minestra   From Italian, meaning a thick soup.

minestrone   A flavorful, thick Italian soup made with a variety of ingredients that usually include vegetables and a starchy food such as rice or pasta.

miroton   A type of French stew made with cooked meat and flavored with onions.

navarin   A French lamb or mutton stew made with small onions and potatoes or with a variety of vegetables.

olla podrida   A hearty national Spanish soup or stew made with a great variety of ingredients, including several kinds of meat.

osso bucco   An Italian stew whose name means literally "hollow bone." Its primary ingredients are veal shanks that are cooked in wine and stock with onions and tomatoes.

oxtail   An ox or beef tail, rich in flavor and highly prized for soups and stews.

petite marmite A famous French dish that comprises clear soup and the meat and vegetables cooked in it. The name is taken from the metal or earthenware pot, *petite marmite*, or small kettle, in which the soup is traditionally cooked and served.

pistou A thick vegetable soup containing pasta; popular in southern France and native to Italy. Its distinctive flavor is derived from a paste of crushed garlic, fresh basil and olive oil.

potage A French word that generally refers to light, often clear, soups.

pot-au-feu A method of preparing soup or stew that yields a clear broth, meat and vegetables, each generally served separately.

purée Food that has been cooked until very soft and then put through a sieve, ricer or blender. Also a thick soup made with puréed vegetables and a liquid.

ragoût A stew of meat, poultry or fish, and sometimes with vegetables, that is generally highly seasoned.

ratatouille A well-seasoned vegetable stew that is popular in Southern France and some other Mediterranean locales. It can be cooked on top of the stove or in the oven.

reduce To cook a liquid over high heat until it is reduced in volume to give it the desired concentrated flavor.

render To melt down a substance such as fat.

roux A mixture of flour and fat cooked together and used to thicken such dishes as soups and stews. For a white *roux* the flour is not cooked until it turns brown as it is for a brown *roux*. A blond *roux* is pale gold and made only with butter.

sauté To brown food in a small quantity of hot fat usually in an open pan or skillet.

sear	To brown the outside of food, especially meats, sealing in the juices and flavors. This is done by frying in hot fat or roasting in a hot oven.
simmer	To cook food gently in a liquid at just below the boiling point, at a temperature of about 185°F.
skim	To remove the accumulated fat and/or scum from the top of a liquid with a slotted spoon or skimmer.
solianka	A piquant Russian soup or stew, usually made with fish and a variety of seasonings.
soup	Meat, poultry, fish, vegetables or a combination of these ingredients, cooked in a seasoned liquid.
soupe	A French word, referring to a hearty, peasant-style soup.
stew	To cook in a liquid, covered, at low heat for a long period of time. A stew can be brown or white. For the former the meat is browned before the liquid is added. For a white stew the meat is put into cold liquid and then heated.
stifado	A Greek stew made with beef or lamb, small white onions, and cooked in a rich garlic and spice-flavored stock.
stock	The rich liquid that is obtained from the simmering together of meat, poultry, seafood, vegetables, and usually some bones, in seasoned water.
thickening agent	One or more foods, such as flour, cornstarch, arrowroot, egg yolk, *beurre manié* or *roux*, used to thicken liquids.
tureen	A covered deep oval or round dish traditionally used for serving soup.

INDEX

1 2 3 4 5 6 7 ← P Y → 9 8 7 6 5